The Science
BEHIND IT

Formulating Success at Any Age

Table of Contents

Dedication & Acknowledgements

You are able to read this book today because of the many people who have helped create the success I have in my own life. I would like to give my heartfelt thanks and gratitude to:

My Dad, James L. Cunningham. The one person in the world that will always tell me straight up any and everything I have ever wanted to know. Always full of awesome intellectual information and knowledge. Thanks dad for being the very best at everything you do for me.

My Mom, Tamara Zantell. She is the wind beneath my wings. Strong, powerful and always ready!

The funniest people I have ever met and the only ones that can light even the darkest days. My grandparents and biggest cheerleaders and prayer warriors, Dr. James A. Lewis III and First Lady Zandra J. Smith-Lewis.

My siblings and best friends: Mercedes, Jimmie Jr, Jimmy and Josiah I'sa.

A surprise, yet well deserving thanks you to Miss. Kemery Oparah. Kemery is the amazing 10-year-old CEO that you will read about in the first chapter of this book. I won't share all the cool parts of her journey, but I will tell you that she personally assisted with the editing of this book. She did a beautiful job. The most magical part of this editing story is that Kemery actually pitched me for the opportunity. How could I say no?

Foreword
By Dr. Ruben West

www.rubenwest360.com
Facebook.com/RubenWestSpeaks

You have no doubt heard the saying "out of the mouths of babes." but for everything a child may say, imagine the countless thoughts and ideas that go unheard, unnoticed and unsupported.

There are many children with great ideas for businesses, products, services and more. Periodically we are introduced to one of these children's success stories shared on the television, in a magazine or newspaper or on some form of social media. We pause and marvel at how "lucky" the kid and/or his or her parents are to have stumbled across this one-of-a-kind opportunity. Often times we never give any real thought or consideration as to the formula behind their success. Was it luck? Are they gifted? Maybe they're just blessed. Could it be all three?

Here is a better question. Have you ever had an idea for a product, service or invention but no idea how to manifest it into reality, so you just let go? Then 6 months, 1 year or 2 years later you see that very same thing, and say out loud, "I thought of that!" Well here's the thing: It's not what you think of, it's what you act on.

In this book, Zandra dispels the myth of success by accident. She highlights 26 young entrepreneurs and the steps they took to bring their brilliance into the marketplace. Obviously, these children couldn't have done it by themselves, but the question remains: How did they do it? Fortunately, this book will reveal the answers. Zandra could have simply shared how she successfully launched her brand, appeared on network television, and is making a difference across the globe. However, she wanted to give inquiring readers multiple ideas and avenues toward success from a variety of individuals who are not just talking about it, but actually doing it.

Prepare to learn, grow and be amazed at how these young moguls detail their personal journeys and the science behind their growth and development.

If you're looking for a book of excuses as to why you, your child or someone you know can't be successful, this is not it! If you hope that by reading this book you will discover that being successful doesn't take personal sweat equity, don't turn the page! However, if you want to discover how resourcefulness as opposed to resources can bring new products, services and businesses into existence regardless of the age, this book is for you!

After reading this book of strategies used by what many would consider to be a group of unlikely entrepreneurs, you will no longer be inclined to focus on the business you see in front of you. You will be compelled to uncover "The Science Behind It".

~ Dr. Ruben M. West

Introduction

"The Science Behind It"

September 2016

Steve Harvey Funderdome

ABC's production studios

I wanted to leave so badly. I was standing in the dressing room that had a couch, fancy snacks, drinks, a desk and a vanity complete with lights all around it. I have my very own dressing room, and, at that, even have a bathroom. As I sat on the couch, planning my escape, I couldn't help but remember that at one point in time, this moment was actually one that I prayed for. This moment was one I had put on my vision board when I was just 10 years old. But even though I had waited for this moment for 6 long years and worked so hard to get here, all I could think about was leaving. By this time, I was freaking out. I was freaking out because at any moment in time, someone was gonna come in, knock on the door to that fancy dressing room and tell me it was my turn to go on stage. You see, I had been selected over thousands and thousands of young people and adults to compete on a live pitch game show called, *The Steve Harvey Funderdome*. It was amazing, yet it was a long, grueling process. Almost a year of interviews, videos, repeating my pitch over and over and over again to many different producers. I remember there being days when I wanted to quit. Like, it almost took me so many days where I thought, "I can't do this anymore." So now that I was there, sitting on a couch, staring at this mirror surrounded by these bright light bulbs, all I could think about was leaving. I told my mom that I was scared. I admit it. I was nervous. Actually, I was freaking out. But you know what? She was scared, nervous and also freaking out. So, we then did the only thing we knew how to do: We called my dad. See, my dad is always the voice of reason. He always knows exactly what to say. This time was no different. My father reminded me that I was in a position that hundreds of thousands or maybe even millions of kids across the world would want to be in. In that very moment, I could not allow my fear to nervously overcome the fact that I had the opportunity to show the world who I really was. I had an amazing

8

opportunity to pitch my business in front of millions of people worldwide. I realized while talking to my dad that I was never going to give up that opportunity because they needed me to show up. These kids needed to know that the dreams they were dreaming were actually possible. Those dreams are possible because we make them possible. I couldn't give up or quit because kids like me are paving the way for other kids every single day. I had ninety seconds to sell hundreds of people in that live audience on my business that I started at 9 years old, Zandra. We're a social good company that educates and empowers girls and women across the globe. We produce plant-based skin care products. I want you to know that I pitched my heart out that day. I pitched for my dad, for my brothers, my sister, my nana and my granddad. I also pitched for you.

Guess what? I won. I won for my mom and my dad. I won for my brothers and my sister. I won for my nana and my granddad. I also won for you. I won because we have something to prove. I won because I was tired of being told, "No." I won because the world needs to know that we are amazing no matter how old or young we are. I won so that I could write this book with 25 other amazing young moguls, so you could read it, and so that you can learn, understand, and execute the science behind our successes. We are here to tell you that you don't have to wait. We are here to give you permission to start today. Not only permission but also some tools, inspiration, guidance and information you need, so you can start today. You no longer have to wait for mom or dad's permission. You no longer have to wait for your teachers to say it's OK. You can start dreaming as huge as you want right now. After reading this book and learning about myself and the other 25 amazing young moguls who wrote this book for you, I hope you will want to start something great and if you've already started, I hope you will be inspired to continue to grow something great. The bottom line is that you already have everything you need. You just need to connect with some young moguls like us so that we can push you along your way. Don't be like me, in that moment, in the dressing room of the show. Don't sit on a couch and wonder if you're good enough. Don't sit on the couch and try to plan your escape; stay, sit and look at yourself in the mirror. Face your fears and charge ahead. If you haven't already figured it out, my name is Zandra.

I am a 17-year-old entrepreneur from Buffalo, N.Y. My fascination with entrepreneurship began when I was 9 years old; inspired by a at the time heartbreaking "no" from my dad. My obsession with lip gloss and lip balm quickly grew out of hand and dad refused to buy me more, suggesting I make my own instead.

My mom enrolled me in the Kids Biz Small Business Development Center program at Buffalo State College just shy of my 10th birthday.

At 13, I became the youngest to ever be accepted and graduate from a University At Buffalo School of Management Center for Entrepreneurial Leadership Program. I spread my wings as a member of several professional organizations, I am very comfortable being the only kid in the room.

Over the last 7 years I have been featured as a TEDx speaker; on several news outlets such as Black Enterprise, NPR, Seventeen Magazine, Teen Boss, Girls Life Magazine, Teen Boss, Forbes, INC, USA TODAY, CNN, Nickelodeon, Essence Magazine, The TODAY Show, Steve Harvey's Funderdome, The Harry Connick Jr. Show, Good Morning America and ABC Nightline and so many others.

I have facilitated workshops/presentations for well-known organizations like BALLE, United Nations, State Colleges, Universities, Girls Scouts USA, Boys and Girls Club, National Public-School systems and Alpha Kappa Alpha and Delta Sigma Theta sororities along with many others.

It's important for me to share all these formalities with you because, I need you to know that there are many components or ingredients that make up each of our success. You journey will be different than mine and mine different from yours but we can both be very successful on our own space. That's what this book is about. I wanted you to see the backend, the truth behind what success looks, feeling and move like.

A little more about me...

I started my creative journey mixing lip balm at my kitchen table. Today, I have a 5000 square foot GMP-compliant production and distribution facility. All Zandra products are handmade in small batches to maintain integrity and quality. As an eco-friendly social good company in Western New York, we are committed to sustainable practices with a priority on how gentle and sensitive teen skin can be. The mission is to create high quality, fun and fresh products that smell amazing but don't have all the unnecessary yucky stuff and chemicals.

There is so much more but you will discover that further into the book.

I recently launched her newest initiatives, Young Mogul Prep School, and The Zandra "TLC" Foundation. One provides coaching to young people on the basics of business, business start-up and how to launch like a pro. The other works to provide entrepreneurial education, experiences and mentorship along with networking opportunities and access to programming that will enhance the lives of young people so they can become change-makers within their families and community

I am Zandra A. Cunningham, and I am the CEO of Zandra. I started my company at 9 years old, so don't ever think that you can't do it. This book is here to guide you. We're gonna help you along the way. You're going to read about all these amazing young moguls who started just like you are. Today, together, we are taking over the world. We all have different kinds of businesses, different kinds of missions and different kinds of purposes, but we are all the same because we are all young moguls. We have all been told, "No," at least one point in time. I hope you enjoy this book. I hope you have an opportunity to read and learn from all 26 young moguls. Reach out to them. Connect with us, because we're here to help you.

Chapter I. Kreativity!
Now, You're Speaking My Language
Kemery Oparah

www.kemeryoparah.com
Facebook.com/kemerykreates
Instagram.com/kemeryoparah
Twitter.com/kemerykreates
Linkedin.com/kemeryoparah

Kemery Oparah, from Atlanta, lives with her mom, dad and 2-year-old brother, Jeremy. Kemery enjoys spending time with her family and teaching her little brother new things. Fluent in Japanese, Kemery has been teaching Jeremy Japanese, too. Kemery loves to dance and has been in two productions of the Urban Nutcracker, put on by Ballethnic Dance Studio. She is currently training for her fourth triathlon, which will be her 21st race. Academically, Kemery is a star student and an avid reader. She has even edited two books.

In January 2017, Kemery and her family were invited by her Japanese teacher to go to Japan. Determined to go, Kemery decided to turn her passion for language and culture into a business. Kemery is the 10-year-old CEO of Kemery Kreates. She began by selling leather bracelets with names and powerful words custom-engraved in Japanese. Kemery later added other types of jewelry to be engraved. Her business has landed her on the cover of *Fayette Woman Magazine* in June 2017, and she was featured in *South Fulton Lifestyles* Magazine in August 2017. Also, in August 2017, Kemery decided to start a clothing line. She and her parents worked hard, teaching themselves the basics of sewing. Kira by Kemery Kreates, Kemery's clothing line, launched in November 2017. Kemery Kreates was chosen as one of the Top 10 business finalists for the HERs OWNly Jr. pitch contest in November 2017. In February 2018, Kemery's clothing line graced the runway of Atlantic City Fashion Week in New Jersey! Kira means "beautiful" in Japanese. Combining her love for fashion and culture, Kemery wants every girl to know they are beautiful. Kemery Kreates is helping others to experience culture through language, design and community.

Kemery currently gives five percent of her revenue to her church and other charities. She is working on other ways to give back to her community, such as teaching Japanese classes online and having sewing playdates where she can teach other children to sew while making items for children in need such as hats for children having surgery, and bags for children in foster care to carry their clothes.

Kemery has a gentle spirit and a dynamic personality. To Kemery, being an author is the next step to broadening her sphere of influence. She wants children to believe that their wildest dreams are able to be achieved if they work hard. "The sky is not the limit. You can go further."
-- Kemery C. Oparah

What is your favorite quote that can be printed on a T-shirt, written on a mirror or wall?

One question that I've been asked is what advice I would give to others. I respond, "The sky is not the limit. You can go further." The bar can never be set too high. As stated by Norman Peale, "Shoot for the moon. Even if you miss, you'll land among the stars." Don't underestimate yourself. Set expectations for yourself higher than you think possible. Give yourself a deadline and push yourself as far as you can. Even if you don't make it, karma will reward you for trying your hardest.

In August 2017 even though I'd only had one week of sewing camp, I came up with the idea for a fashion line. We submitted for Atlantic City Fashion Week as a long shot to produce seven different outfits. The fashion show asked us if we could do 15 outfits instead. We agreed, although we had no idea how it was even going to be possible. Somehow, we left for Atlantic City with a rack full of 15 outfits ready for the runway. On the day of the show during dress rehearsals, one of the designers couldn't make it, so there were a few child models who needed clothes to model. The organizers asked if I could come up with three more designs. With some brainstorming and some little miracles we pulled off 18 outfits for 2018 Atlantic City Fashion Week and the show was ABSOLUTELY AMAZING! It just goes to show that we were able to go further than we believed possible.

What are the 6 major ingredients or components that have contributed to the formulation of your success as a young change-maker thus far?

Ingredient number one is knowing my original idea, as well as knowing where I am currently in my business. You can never know where you're going unless you know where you started. I started with leather bracelets that were custom-engraved in Japanese. Now I'm developing online courses to teach other children how to speak Japanese.

Ingredient number two is knowing my short-term and long-term goals. Now that I know where I am and where I've been, I need to know where I want to be. For instance, in the next 3 years, I would like to teach 500 people to speak Japanese, sew or start their own business. I can reach more people by teaching and training.

Ingredient number three is doing prior research on events and programs and knowing what to expect. It helps to know what kind of people will be at vending opportunities so that you can tweak your pitch to match their interests. That way, customers think that you were just what they were looking for.

Ingredient number four is standing in front of my booth and talking to customers even if they don't talk to me first. Sometimes, in fact, most of the time, potential customers will ignore you, or pretend that they don't see you, and try to walk past you. One way to keep that from happening is to step in front and start talking so that they have to stop and make it obvious that they heard you.

Ingredient number five is having a few different price ranges so that even kids can buy something. Have a low-priced, middle-priced, and high-priced item available to accommodate customers with varying budgets. Remember, sometimes you may be vending at a children's event and children do not always have a lot of money to spend, but still want to buy something from you.

Ingredient number six is having the same smile for every customer. At the end of the work day you probably feel exhausted, but don't let it get to you because sometimes the best customers come after the event is over. Sometimes another vendor finally gets a chance to stop by your booth, and they'd like to make a purchase before they leave.

What does your typical business or work day look like? When do you fit in fun, school, friends and family?

The night before a vending event is normally spent going through our supplies making sure we have everything we need. Once we have found and packed up everything, we set up our Square app for the next day's event. I set my alarm clock depending on what I need to do in the morning, how long it should take, what time the event is and how far away it is. In the morning, I wake up, get ready for the day, and talk to my parents about the details of the event. During the car ride there, I compose what I am going to say. At the location, we scope out the layout of the event, then set up our table and sometimes our tent. Then we talk to as many potential customers as possible. As we make sales, we try to stay as organized as possible. After the last sale, we break down the booth, load up the vehicle and stop somewhere for a treat on the way back home.

On non-business days I go to school and hang out with my friends. In my free time, I love to read, play with my baby brother and hang out with my friends and family.

What would you say success means to you? Why is it so important?

Some say the meaning of success is having achieved a goal. Once you are successful in reaching one goal, you should give yourself another, as you can never set the bar too high. Therefore, you're never fully successful, you should always have a goal to reach. So I believe success is the process of growth as you set goals, achieve them and then set new goals.

Recently I received a proclamation from the City of South Fulton. Just hearing my achievements read out loud helped me realize that even though I haven't made it to Japan yet, I am still being successful.

How important would you say it is to be connected to other young people doing amazing things? How did you make these connections?

Oprah Winfrey says, "You must surround yourself with people who lift you higher." If you don't know anyone, then you don't know who to go to when you need help. So, you need to meet as many people as possible. I do this by attending many events and doing my very best to talk to different people there. You never know who you're talking to, so never dull your shine. This means that you must be the best possible version of you, no matter who you think you're talking to, because you may be completely surprised.

How important would you say reading and research is to the success of your business? What 3 business books would you recommend?

I think it is very important to research and read books because even though some of your business you must figure out on your own, you still need to know where to start. It's also helpful to have some tips along the way.

We don't usually watch much television at our house, but you might be able to guess that one of our favorite shows to watch is "Shark Tank." We watched it even before starting my business. Before, it was just entertaining, and we would anticipate which shark would want "in" on the deal, or which shark would say they were "out" first. After starting Kemery Kreates, we watch Shark Tank differently. Now, we listen to the numbers to see if they make sense. Are they asking for a reasonable amount of money given the stake in the company they are offering? We listen to find out their sales in relation to the time they have been in business. What will they do with the investment? I read a book from the shark who started a fashion company and drove it to success with hard work. Daymond John said in his book, ***Rise and Grind***, "The time will never be perfect, so you can only make perfect use of your time." This is great advice for running both a business and your daily life. It's important to make good use of your time. If you work hard effectively, you will also have time to play hard. He also gave the advice to, "Dream small." Setting small goals seems much easier to achieve than when you have an end goal that seems monstrous!

Deepak Chopra shared The Law of Least Effort in his book, ***The Seven Spiritual Laws of Success***, which helped me to learn that there are times when it's good to do everything the hard way, but there are also other times when we need to work smarter, not harder.

TaVona Denise talks about The Cure for Fear in her book, **Unstoppable Success**. She describes the cure for fear as, "When I try something, I like to think of it like a science experiment. I form a hypothesis. ... Using this approach turns off emotion enough for you to get into action, you're just being curious. I wonder what would happen if ...?" This is useful when you're about to do something intimidating. As I train for my fourth triathlon, this advice keeps me from psyching myself out and helps me to stay focused!

If you could advise a future young mogul to do 3 things before starting their business what would they be?
Find your passion and think of a business that suits it. Think about what you like to do for fun. Then think about what you do for fun that requires the least amount of materials and time to make a lot of that item. Consider what would you like to do repeatedly, even if you never got paid for it. If you like to bake, you might sell pastries. If you like to do crafts, such as painting, knitting, sewing, etc, you could sell your creations. Maybe you are into soccer. You could write a book about soccer or help coach younger children with basic skills like dribbling and passing the ball, and basic exercises to help with running during a game.

The second thing you should do is find the people who will support your business the most and advertise toward them. They are your target audience. I have a pitch that I am very familiar with using in most situations. Depending on the audience, I change my pitch. One thing that I have learned is that my product is not for every customer. In the beginning, we went to many different vending events. We still go to many events, but now we pick events that may have the audience we want to reach. In the past, I went to one event where the community really values education and used my typical approach of introducing myself in Japanese first and then in English. At another event, clearly the audience there was not as into the language. When I switched to greeting the customers in English first, I reached more customers for the remainder of the event. I know my product is for children, so I may have a bubble-maker at my booth, but adults pay for products. Children like to feel noticed, too. I do. Don't you? When a child comes to you, talk with them and get them engaged.

The last thing you should do before starting a business is to find events that cater to your target audience. Make sure that the events you attend are a good match for the personality of your business and your target audience. I may not want to sell my tutus at a monster truck rally. The sales may not be where I want them for the day. But everyone loves slime! You could sell it at a cheerleading competition or a monster truck rally! If you make your own board games, you may have success vending at a children's business fair, but less success vending at an adult business convention.

What are 3 lessons you have learned so far as a CEO, founder or public figure?

You must be assertive, or people won't take you seriously, because you are a child.

If you stand behind the table, people can easily walk past you. One lesson I learned from Maisha S. Wynn's book, *The Wynning Way*, is that "[I] only have seven seconds to make a good first impression." One time while I was out supporting another young mogul, someone else was also supporting her and that someone else was a friendly woman who happens to be a popular personality for the local radio station. Even though I didn't know she would be there, I didn't let that catch me off-guard. I made sure I was confident and approached her. One thing led to another and I was on the radio a couple of days later, telling my story to all of her listeners. One way I can be assertive is to actively move toward the conversation instead of shy away and lean on my display table. My mom always reminds me to speak "loud, strong, and powerful so my ancestors can hear me." To me, it feels like I am yelling, but many times I need to be that loud because there are other things going on at events like music playing in the background, other vendors and customers talking, people on their phones, maybe airplanes flying by if we are outside, etc. A good sign that you may not be speaking as loudly as you think you are is if the customer has to lean in closer to get their ear closer to the sound of your voice.

Make prices higher than what it costs you to produce your product or service, but low enough that customers can afford to pay for it. You aren't just selling your product, you're selling your story. If your product is one that a customer could make on their own or could be bought somewhere else, they are really buying it because they believe in you and want to support you. They believe in your story.

18

Where do you pull inspiration from?

I pull my inspiration from culture, many different cultures. In this case, I have been focused on Japan. I have been learning Japanese since I was 13 months old. I am really fascinated with the culture, the language, the food and the fashion in Japan. I started my business to raise money for my first trip to Japan, and even have an Asian-inspired clothing line called Kira. Kira means "beauty" in Japanese.

One of the things I love about Japanese culture is the traditional and pop music. I love making food with my Japanese teacher. She has helped me and my friends to make dongo, dumplings, sushi, and other Japanese dishes. She has also shown me how to make onigiri, which is kind of rice. Now my family and I can make onigiri at home. Of course, I like having a fun language that my friends and I can speak. I've been teaching my brother, Jeremy, to speak Japanese. One day, Jeremy and I will be able to speak Japanese together, too.

What are 3 specific challenges you have had as a young mogul? How have you been able to overcome them?

Obstacles will come up. Challenges will happen. You have to anticipate problems before they happen. Assume that you will need multiple methods of receiving payment. People will tell you they do not have cash. Be their solution. Let them know you accept payment via card, PayPal, or whatever methods you have available. If you sell baseball cards and they only like basketball, invite them to buy a gift for a friend, or make sure you have that tip jar close by so they can leave a tip if they want to support your story but are not interested in the product you are selling. If they have a problem, find a way to be their solution, if possible. In the case that your product or service is not a good match for the customer, remember to smile, ask them to tell a friend who may be interested, and thank them for their time.

You have to be prepared to handle problems that could not be anticipated. In September 2017, before my biggest vending event of the year, I broke my arm! Since I was still in the hospital at 3 a.m. on the day of the event, my parents let the venue know that I would not be able to attend. Fortunately, it was a two-day event. The first day, we went as spectators and touched base with the person in charge. On day two we set up and even with my arm in a cast, I still had the second biggest selling day of the year! I had to enlist the help of my parents. Fortunately, they are fairly good artists and could copy the characters that I showed them in a book. I checked for quality control and we rocked that event, literally with one arm tied ... just not behind my back.

Many times, events do not have a lot of customers. One way you can help yourself and help build relationships with companies is to help promote events that are hosting you as a vendor. Help get people to the event to help make the event a success as well as increase your sales. When you do go to an event that does not have a lot of customers, use the opportunity to network with other vendors and the customers who attend the event. This is how I met someone who arranged a private tour of Pinewood Studios for my Mom and I while they were filming the pilot season of a new show. She arranged for me to meet with the show's costume designer and get a sneak peek of behind the scenes as a costume designer. Pinewood Studios is one of the premiere movie studios in the country and that experience was amazing! We even had ice cream and got to each lunch with the cast and crew.

What are your goals for the future? What's next?
Long-term goals:

Communication: I plan to expand my Japanese courses and entrepreneur class to provide a variety of opportunities for children to grow their talents in this area.

Design: For my clothing line, Kira by Kemery Kreates, I want girls to have fun and stylish clothes that help them feel comfortable and beautiful.

Community: I plan to increase my charitable donations from 5 percent to 10 percent as my business grows. I want to be able to give back to my community and help other children to be successful.

Personally: I want my business to be able to bring in enough money to pay for college and help me to buy a house with enough land for a horse. I would also love to travel to all 50 states and six of the seven continents.

Short term goals:

Communication: I started my business to take my first trip to Japan. I'm definitely going to get there. You can follow me on Facebook and Instagram to see pictures from the trip. I am completing the Japanese course and preparing to run my first pilot study. Exciting!

Design: I was invited to participate in Atlantic City Fashion Week and New York City Fashion this year. We could not attend this time but hope to have the opportunity to showcase again next year. For now, I will continue to sew and create for fashion shows and custom orders. I will expand the design part of the business after our Japanese courses and entrepreneur courses are running smoothly ... unless we obtain seed funding to help with the growth.

Community: Within the next three years, my goal is to help 500 children to successfully complete my Hiragana course, learn to sew or be encouraged start their own business by taking one of my courses, workshops, hearing me speak at an assembly or by reading this book!

Another short-term goal is to prepare and pitch my first big marketing proposal to a major company.

I am Kemery C. Oparah, a 10-year old CEO, and I started my business at 8 years old. My mission is to help children everywhere to experience culture through communication, design and community. In my business, I help children and teens to learn skills they may need on their life journey, like speaking another language, designing and creating their own clothes, turning their passion and talents into profit and having a heart to give back to the community. I am also a reader, a friend, an athlete, a polygot and a dreamer. I hope to inspire you to always have the desire to learn something new.

ACKNOWLEDGEMENTS

A very special thank you to those who have supported my journey

and helped me turn my dreams into a reality...

Mommy, Daddy, and Jeremy; Ace and Linda Haselrig "Grandaddy & Grandmommy"; Dr. & Mrs. Bernard and Dawn Oparah "Grandma & Grandpa"; Amadi Leadership Associates, Inc.; James, Erika, Sean, and Kaitlyn Williams; Kelechuwu, Anna, Ogechi, and Chinonso Oparah; Eric and Marcia Mayhand; Betty Oliver & Great-Gran; Cousin Larry; Joy Burton; Jimmy and Jackie Wilson; Bobby and Jacqueline Allen; The Marks Family; OMNI International School; Mayu Edwards; Dr. Tyler S. Thigpen; Tamla Oates-Forney; Gracyn Thompson; Chloe Love; The Miller Family

Chapter II. Don't Judge A Book
King Josiah I'sa

www.kingjosiahisa.com
Facebook.com/KingJosiahI'sa
Instagram.com/KingJosiahI'sa

King Josiah I'sa Cunningham is a jewelry designer, author and athlete. He wrote and published his first book at 13 years old. As a creative education advocate, Josiah struggled early in the mainstream school system. Disciplinary action, IEPs, labels and let downs were a part of his norm. Having a strong support system in his parents led him to a better understanding of how his way of learning wasn't wrong; instead, it was simply different. Josiah's learning skills seemed so unique, it left educators unsure on how to inspire his success. After years of a sensory and A.D.D. diagnoses along with daily medications that never seemed quite right, Josiah made a decision to no longer allow others' lack of patience, a defeated attitude and embarrassment hold him back.

It wasn't until he truly comprehended the meaning of his name that life changed. Josiah realized he had a higher purpose and mission. Biblically, Josiah became King of Judah at the age of 8. This inspired Josiah to want to take on a leadership role in his own life. He learned early on that as a leader, he could create awareness and be a support system for other children who have been misunderstood and misdiagnosed.

Josiah is a quiet voice for those kids out there who feel as though because they may not be as gifted as their peers academically, they can't have an amazing, successful life. He is here to tell them that they still have value to contribute to the world, and they, too, can live amazing lives full of opportunity and become change-makers.

What is your favorite quote that can be printed on a T-shirt, written on a mirror or wall?

My favorite quote is, "The sky's the limit: You can do anything you put your mind to," however, I recently read a quote that makes me feel even more empowered. The quote was, "How is the sky the limit when there are footprints on the moon?" That quote is powerful beyond measure. It takes the original quote, often used too much to be interesting or thoughtful, to a statement that is now proven. I really can go beyond the sky!

What are the 6 major ingredients or components that have contributed to the formulation of your success as a young change-maker thus far?

- Research – You must do your research! Research leads to mastery. If you want people to take you seriously, you can't pretend to know your craft. People want to feel confident you know exactly what you are talking about. My dad once told me that it takes at least 10,000 hours of engagement/experience/research of a subject to become an expert on that subject. If a person is engaged in their subject for 10 hours per day, it will take a little less than 3 years to become an expert. This is why, if you want to become an expert or a master of something, research a subject you are in love with, otherwise, you will become a jack of that trade and a master of nothing.

- Family – Family support is often underrated. Without my family support, I wouldn't be as successful as I am. Family is usually the first to believe in our crazy dreams and ideas. Family is the least likely to unfavorably judge us. Family is the only group of people that will be honest with you (good or bad), but not kill your spirit. Family will do everything to keep us on the path of success and not let us slack. Most of all, family will teach us the pitfalls and how to avoid them; however, if we do stray from their teachings and fall, family will only look down on us to help us back up.

- Discipline – Having the ability to give up the things I want to do in order to do the things I need to do for success has been very important. I watched my older sister, Zandra, exercise great discipline with her business. We are only one year apart but she has had a lot more experience that I have in business. Although I am not where she is in discipline, her discipline inspires me to keep doing, and to sacrifice a nap for the dream.

- Commitment – I agree to do what I said I will do. I believe a man is only as good as his word. Keeping my word is very important to me. I heard one of the greatest quotes of about commitment ever! The quote said, "Commitment is doing the things you said you will do long after the feeling in which you said it has passed." A lot of people lose their commitment once they encounter a tough time. Not me, I will always remember. tough people last and tough times don't.

- Networking – I don't know everything, but I look to connect with people who know more than I do. My dad told me a quote that took me a while to understand, but now I do understand. He said, "In order to know everything, you must allow yourself to learn thereafter." What I have learned from this quote from my dad is that the smartest and most successful person will always allow themselves to be taught more than what they already know. This is why I will do my best to network with others for that purpose.

- Learning me - I had to learn who I was. I couldn't expect my teachers and family to understand me if I didn't understand me. I had to spend time reading and watching other men and community leaders that I wanted to be more like. My father and grandfather were great examples of what I wanted my life to look like. I knew that if I wanted to be successful I need to learn what success looks like for me, what would make me happy. Once you figure out what your success looks like you can then surround yourself with people, information and experiences that will only support and develop it.

What does your typical business or work day look like? When do you fit in fun, school, friends and family?

My typical business day is long. I wake up and do my morning routine, which consists of getting cleaned up and going to school. After school, I go to work as the production assistant at my sisters company and our family business, Zandra. My job consists of sanitation, organization and making sure the production and classroom spaces are fit for inspection. I take pride in my role. I know that by doing the best I can each day and at times going above and beyond will set me up for other opportunities within the company.

24

I am working on a project where I will be able to incorporate my jewelry design into another brand of the company. It important that I work on my design ideas as i want to grow my business and sell more pieces.

On the days I get out early from work or I am off, I might play my XBox or PlayStation game until dinner is ready. After dinner, I will wind down by either watching something on Netflix or reading about diamonds, gems and precious metals that I like to work with.

What would you say success means to you? Why is it so important?

Winning is what success means to me. I don't like to be in last place. The reason success is so important to me is that success has been taught by my family since I was born. The key to real success is being able to do something that someone else either wouldn't or couldn't do.

I have been told for years, all the things I can't do. Now, I am determined to show the world that I can do anything and everything I put my heart and mind to. The idea of building my jewelry business and standing on stages to share my story really excites me. I know I have a story to tell that other kids and some adults need to hear. Success for me right now is growing my personal brand with integrity and being someone other young men can look up to as an example and alternative to what society tells us we are or we have to be.

How important would you say it is to be connected to other young people doing amazing things? How did you make these connections?

I think it is very important to be connected with other young people doing amazing things, if I am doing amazing things. No one wants to feel weird about being amazing. I have made a lot of connections through my sister Zandra. She is so successful, and she introduces me to some of her successful and amazing friends. We keep the connection alive. I have taken what I have learned from Zandra and passed it down to some of my friends, and now they want to be entrepreneurs as well.

How important would you say reading and research is to the success of your business? What business books would you recommend?

Reading and research are very important to having a successful business. Especially if you are presenting your business to someone. You must know your business inside and out.

I suggest reading books by Warren Buffett, ***Think Big Act Small*** by Jason Jennings, and ***The Culture Code*** by Daniel Coyle

If you could advise a future young mogul important things before starting their business, what would they be?

I would advise them:

- Do your research - As I stated earlier, become a master or an expert in your field. Provide the comfort level satisfactory to the people you meet and speak with.

- Find the love in what you are doing - I know this one seems easy, but it's not. Finding the love in what you are doing is often missed by so many people. Only truly successful people will find the love in what they are doing. How many successful entrepreneurs are upset about going into something they have built and made grow out of love and sacrifice? Usually, the only time a successful entrepreneur is upset about what they have made is when it comes time to share it with an investor.

- Don't be afraid to be different. I have learned to embrace my differences and you will too. Different turns heads, different gets invited back and different will always start a conversation. I walk in the room and people don't know what to think. You know what? I'm cool with that because I need them to meet me as I am and know that I am a young, intelligent, educated black man that can hold a conversation and anything you want. I am here to change the way you view and feel about young, black, gold chain wearing men with locs. I show up different and I am perfectly okay with that.

- Be coachable - My dad is an expert football and wrestling coach, and he told me there is nothing worse to a coach than having an uncoachable person on the team. This is about character, not about talent. If you are not able to learn anything new from someone else -- perhaps an already-made expert -- then you may miss out on your success; at least consistent success. As Vince Lombardi once said, "Talent can get you to the top, but it will be your character that will keep you there."

What are 3 lessons you have learned so far as a CEO, founder or public figure?

I've learned that it's hard running a business, because it takes so much time and commitment to make it become successful. Running a business is sometimes lonely, despite being around people often. When the people leave, it's just you. This is why being around like-minded people is very important, because they share similar thoughts, which proves you are not alone.

I have also learned you must have patience. They say Rome wasn't built in a day. To be successful takes a lot of time; this is the main reason it is important to stay committed to your dream and not exchange it for a nap. Whenever I start to become a bit impatient, I remind myself that God, the most powerful of all-time, took six days to create the heavens and the earth, which is far more difficult than what I am doing.

Lastly, the third lesson I have learned is that you must have a good attitude. I learned this lesson by watching Zandra perform. Although I know she is tired and drained, she performs with a great attitude. People respect that about her, and I want them to have the same respect for me. I know I still must earn it that respect, and I will. Zandra has always been a pro. Zandra will perform her best regardless of how she feels inside. Now that's respect!

Where do you pull inspiration from? Person, place or thing

I pull my inspiration from my family and friends. They make me happy and remind me to be successful. However, if I had to just pull from one person, I would have to say Zandra. The way she handles herself and her business is fascinating to me. I am extremely happy I have a front-row seat to watching her perform.

What are 3 specific challenges you have had as a young mogul? How have you been able to overcome them?

The three challenges that I've had over the last year was first, finishing school. Business success starts with academic achievement; therefore, it was very important I successfully balance school and my business. I was able to overcome this challenge by being disciplined with studying. Realizing my ultimate goal of success requires academic achievement, I remained committed to finishing school at the top.

Secondly, finishing school is not enough, it was important to me to do well in school and not just enough to complete. It was important to me to overcome the nervousness in doing well with my exams. During exam week, I focused on my school subjects a lot. I didn't allow outside distractions to interfere with my goal. I am happy to report that I have overcome the first two challenges. However, my third challenge remains in progress.

My third challenge is getting people to see me for who I really am. You see, I don't look like what people imagine an artist, author or advocate to look like. I have locs, wear a ton of jewelry and I have my fair share of swag. My appearance to many comes with a preconceived idea of who I am and what I stand for. The looks I get, the thoughts people have when they see me as a young black man walk into the room. That I cannot control. It's a challenge. The way I am overcoming that is by being my authentic self, presenting well and shocking the socks off them when I look them in the eye and start to speak. I want my work as a change agent to speak for me and other young men out there that always just need the much-needed opportunity to sit at the table.

What are your goals for the future? What's next?

My goals for next year are to finish high school with great grades. I want to be accepted into any college of my choice. I want my business to do very well. I would like to at least have a prototype of my product available within the next year. Most importantly, I want to make my family proud of me and my accomplishments; especially Zandra.

I am King Josiah I'sa and I started my business at 16 years old. My mission is to create really creative jewelry that my peers would be proud to wear. I am using my platform to bring awareness to an educational system that wasn't built for students like me, the creative learner. I have a strong opinion, huge value to bring to the world and a stand in the gap for other young people that struggle daily to be successful in school. I want them to know they can learn, they will be successful and there is nothing wrong with learning differently.

28

ACKNOWLEDGEMENTS

A very special thank you to those who have supported my journey and helped me turn my dreams into a reality...

My Nana and Grandad; Aunt Tempthia "Kim" Battle; Trevor Battle; My little cousin Sydney Battle; My Godmother Catherine Williams Robinson; Uncle Frank Cunningham; Uncle Willie "Jay" Cunningham; Uncle Willie "Junior" Cunningham; Ms. Janel Jones; Christon "The Truth" Jones; Aunt Mary Wilson; Aunt Martha "Linda"; Aunt Ikeshia Fields; Uncle Leonard Fields; Ms. Vanessa Turner; Aunt Cheryl Williams-Manney; Aunt Stephanie Williams; Aunt Rachel Cunningham; Aunt Christine Cunningham; Coach Brodnicki; Coach Gemmer. Special thanks to my brothers LJ, James, Will and my sisters Mercedes and Zandra.

Chapter III. Secrets of Stephanie Friends and Fashion
Stephanie E. Smith

www.sass-e-todds.com
Facebook.com/sassetodds
Instagram.com/sassetodds
Twitter.com/sassetodds
Linkedin.com/company/sass-e-todds

Stephanie E. Smith is a natural fashionista and trendsetter. She is a Chicago native and loves all things hair, fashion and style. Early on, Stephanie was very shy and struggled with separation anxiety. She found her voice through creative design and the arts. She is 7 years old and enjoys singing, dancing and playing with her little sister and business partner, Samantha.

In 2017 Stephanie co-founded fashion brand SASS-E Todd's with her sister Samantha. SASS-E Todd's is short for **S**tephanie and **S**amantha **S**mith **E**mpower **T**oddlers. The company's mission is to inspire little ones everywhere to reach for the stars and follow their dreams. SASS-E Todd's online boutique features bold and bright apparel designed by Stephanie and Samantha. The girls are actively involved in every aspect of the company and are excited to see their creations come to life and become real items for sell.

Stephanie has been featured on Megyn Kelly Today, WGN TV Chicago's Very Own, Marie Claire Magazine and a host of international publications. She loves making beautiful fashions and hopes to one day help kids that don't have the clothes they need.

What is your favorite quote that can be printed on a T-shirt, written on a mirror or wall?

My favorite quote is "So pretty, So sparkly". My other favorite quote is "That's so Fashion".

What are the 6 major ingredients or components that have contributed to the formulation of your success as a young change-maker thus far?

The six main ingredients for success are one, practicing. I keep drawing and drawing and drawing. And each time, my outfits come out prettier and prettier. Number two, conquer your fears. It's okay. Don't be scared. There's nothing to be afraid of. Just give it a try. If it doesn't go the way you want, you can do it again. If you have to do it five times, then do it five times. If you have to do it fifteen times, then do it fifteen times. If you have to do it 100 times, then do it 100 times. And if you get scared, and if you get sad, you can be sad for a little bit, but you have to try again. Number three, just be nice. What if people don't like you? What if people don't believe in you? You have to ignore people that say mean things. I do not want to hear mean words. If you have something mean to say, then just don't say it. Just be nice. Number four, love God. God is great. He is really awesome and great. He made all of us. He is very helpful and nice and makes rainbows. Rainbows are my favorite color because all the colors of the rainbow are beautiful, sparkly and shiny. I love how God helps people and takes care of them. He takes care of our loved ones even those who passed away. God has done a lot of things for me. God has done a lot of things for me. He makes me have power and He lets me live a good life. I love my pastor. I think he's a great pastor. Number five, family. All of my family members are great, and I love spending time with them. My Grandma Patterson helps me with my homework. She helps me with math and science. She helps me not to be shy. She shows me how to cook bacon and sausages and rice. She helps me with SASS-E Todds' photoshoots and poses. She helps me not to be scared. My Grammy helps me to cook and fix things. She teaches me how to be helpful. She teaches me how to be nice. She helps me with my clothes. And she helps me figure out how to sew and tighten my clothes with pins. My Mema also teaches me to sew with a sharp needle without poking myself. Mommy and Daddy help me not to be shy. Mommy helps me to be helpful. I help my mommy to work out because being fit is important. My sister, Samantha, is a great cutie little sister. All of my family is on my side. They will always be by my side and I would never lose. Number six, helping others. I want to help people not to be homeless. I want people to have lots of food and clothing. I want them to have a home with windows, clean bathrooms and a neighborhood with a soft bed. I want to help people do their chores and help them earn money.

What does your typical business or work day look like? When do you fit in fun, school, friends and family?

I like to draw when I'm not watching TV or kid's shows. I like to draw in the morning and at nighttime before bed. I also like to draw with my sister. We like making outfits together so we are not alone. I like to help my sister Samantha draw her clothing and color inside the lines. I like to travel to New York and around the world to tell people about SASS-E Todd's and my clothes. I am saving my money for a house with 49 bathrooms so that there is room for everyone and we don't have to take turns when there's an emergency. I want a mansion house in California.

What would you say success means to you? Why is it so important?

The things that would make me really happy, because being happy is being successful are moving to California, having a really, really big mansion and being with my family and friends. That's what success, also known as happiness, looks like to me. Success and happiness is having a house on the beach where I can make sand castles with my friends.

How important would you say it is to be connected to other young people doing amazing things? How did you make these connections?

This is important to me because I want to be nice and kind to everyone. When people are happy, they are not bullies. It is important to share with my sister and business partner. Sharing is caring. You have to work really hard and help others and never give up. When big kids help, that helps a lot because they know more than little kids. They are smarter because they are older. Learning new things and working together helps you to make new friends. And that makes me feel amazing and happy. I make new friends and connect by being nice to them. When I meet a new friend, I introduce myself. I say, "Hello. My name is Stephanie, and how are you doing?" And I ask them to be my friend.

How important would you say reading and research is to the success of your business? What 3 business books would you recommend?

My three favorite books are **Hercules**, **Frozen** and **Goodnight Moon**. They are my favorite books because they are colorful and they are not boring. Reading books is important, but just get started.

If you could advise a future young mogul to do 3 things before starting their business what would they be?

Number one, it's a really hard job and you have to make sure you get everything perfect. Number two, you have to work hard and keep trying. Just keep coloring. And number three, you have to work every single day when you feel like it. And when you don't feel like it, take a break and do something else fun.

What are 3 lessons you have learned so far as a CEO, founder or public figure?

It taught me a lot of things. It taught me how to draw inside the lines. It taught me how to carefully use color and not mix too much. It taught me how to talk to people, how to be a great artist and how to tell stories. I learned more words. It taught me you need to be smart, helpful, kind and trusting.

Where do you pull inspiration from? Person, place or thing

I am inspired by my thoughts. I get my ideas from my head. My brain knows everything about me and it tells my mouth what to do. When I go outside and see trees and flowers, I feel the fresh air and it makes me calm. When I travel and go places. it makes me feel at home. I like seeing outfits and fashion in other countries. I think they are pretty and cute and amazing. I've been to New York, Jamaica, Germany and all over the country. I love fashion.

What are 3 specific challenges you have had as a young mogul? How have you been able to overcome them?

Sometimes it takes a really long time for people to buy our clothes. We have sold a lot of clothes, but I want to sell more; enough to be in a mansion. That is a lot of waiting and it takes a lot of time to get people to know who you are. I don't want to quit. I want to keep trying. It won't take too long as long as you focus. Focusing helps me not to panic. It helps me not to get too scared. It allows me to breathe in and breathe out. It helps me to be brave. I know I have my parents, so I'm not scared.

What are your goals for the future? What's next?

I would like to see my family and my friends wearing my SASS-E Todd's clothes in the future. I also want to travel to other places while our factories make clothes. I also want other kids to learn how to be a real fashion designer. You have to work really hard and never give up. You always have to practice.

I want to tell them if you wanna be a fashion designer, you always have to strike a really pretty pose at a photoshoot or a picture place.

I am Stephanie Erin Smith of SASS-E Todds, and I started my business when I was 6 years old. My mission is to inspire kids everywhere to do what they love. I make cute and colorful clothes that are extra comfy and have pictures that look like all kids. I love meeting new people and modeling my fashions. I want to teach more kids how to design clothes and bring them to life!

ACKNOWLEDGEMENTS

A very special thank you to those who have supported my journey

and helped me turn my dreams into a reality...

Grandpa William Patterson; Grandma Laura Patterson; Mommy; Daddy; Samantha M. Smith; Rebecca Richmond; Karen Lewis; Hope LeNoir, Expert Career Coach, Brandy Watkins; Grammy Sherlyn; Stephen H. Smith; Veronica Seyoum; Chanel Strong; Cherie Johnson; Tamiko Dockery; Soleil and Giselle Foucher; Kristi Tunstall; Letitia Dillard-Birks; Elethia Tillman; Shuntae Williams

Chapter IV. A Taste of Heaven!
Daara & Demilade Olaniyan

www.thedreambasketdelights.com
Facebook.com/thedreambasketdelights
Instagram.com/thedreambasketdelights
Twitter.com/the_dreambasket

Oluwadaara and Oluwademilade Olaniyan, ages 11 and 8 years old are two multiple award winning and enterprising sisters who are extremely passionate about baking and cooking. "Daara and Demilade", as they are popularly known, are young entrepreneurs who own "The Dream Basket Delights", a Sweet Treats and Delights company that specializes in custom cakes, pies, finger foods, light meals and a variety of desserts. They live in Lagos and are from the Southwestern region of Nigeria in West Africa.

Their business was started as a result of their great passion and love for baking in particular and a unique interest in food in general, which had been inherent from early childhood and encouraged by inspiration from their mum.

The sisters jointly have the responsibilities of researching and innovating new recipes as well as sales and marketing of their products and services.

Daara and Demilade have been featured on several media platforms and publications, which include The Guardian Newspaper, an independent daily newspaper published in Lagos, as "Kid Entrepreneurs" in the business segment of the publication.

Also, the resourceful sisters have been interviewed on the Pan African Entertainment and Lifestyle Television Network, EbonyLife TV's flagship show "Moments Nigeria" on DSTV Channel 165, which distributes content to 49 African countries, including South Africa and Southern African countries.

Other features include Nunu Milk PLC, a PZ Cussons brand for food and nutrition as Nunu Smartkids and the Kids of the Cosmos (KOTK), a children's school supply and story brand inspired by kids and their achievements in the United States.

In 2017, they won the award for the "Most Independent Kid Entrepreneur Prize" at the KENT fair. In June 2018, they won the "Entrepreneur of the Year 2018" award by the Child Summit and Award Organization. It is also important to state that the sisters are ambassadors for the Kidpreneur Africa Organization.

Daara and Demilade are multi-talented young moguls with interests in languages, sports and music. They play at least two musical instruments each, including the guitar, piano and violin.

What is your favorite quote that can be printed on a T-shirt, written on a mirror or wall?

Our mission is to inspire other children all over the world to follow their passion and dream big, which could lead them to becoming change-makers or entrepreneurs.

Our favorite quote which has encouraged us through our journey of entrepreneurship is "Never doubt yourself for a minute, and keep pushing forward, because with focus and positivity, the sky is not even the limit."

What are the 6 major ingredients or components that have contributed to the formulation of your success as a young change-maker thus far?

There are many components that have contributed to the formulation of our success as young change-makers. Our six major ones include the following:

36

- God - God is the center of our success story, because he has given us life, blessed us with unique talents and has made all opportunities possible for us to come this far.

- Inspiration - Our inspiration comes from shared ideas between us and our mom, as well as from our early childhood. We also get inspired from the works of our favorite chefs/bakers who have been in the industry long before us.

- Motivation - We are motivated to improve on our skills and craft by the encouragement and support from our parents, customers, friends, family and organizations who have acknowledged and recognized our talents.

- Support - As young entrepreneurs, support is a very essential part of our success story.
  We have been blessed to have an exceptional support system from our parents, family, friends, customers, well-wishers and admirers.

- Passion - Our passion for baking and cooking has been a major component in formulating our success. It is the passion that has kept us going through the tough times.

- Ambition - Our hunger for success has constantly propelled us to always challenge ourselves by going the extra mile and put our very best in our business all the time.

What does your typical business or work day look like? When do you fit in fun, school, friends and family?

Our schedule could be generally tedious but with the help of our mom as our manager, we always work things out. It's important to state that for us school is a very high priority, and as such, our schedules are planned around our school work and activities.

This is because having a solid educational background is a key component required for the achievement and sustenance of success.

We start our weekdays by getting ready for school. At school, we have the normal schedule as structured in our various schools. After school, we attend to our homework and once that is completed, we can have leisure time during which we have quality time with family and friends, or work on our business by either fulfilling orders and deliveries, or trying out new recipes, or attending to paperwork.

Lastly, we have our dinner and go to bed with a target of getting to bed early.

On weekends, we start our day by attending workouts and exercises at the gym. Saturdays are always fun, because we get a break from the usual weekday hustle and relax, too.

Thereafter, we plan our homework schedule for the weekend and review our business commitments in terms of outstanding orders and paperwork. Sundays are also very different, because we are closed for business and get ready for a fresh new week ahead.

What would you say success means to you? Why is it so important?

The word "success" means different things to different people depending on their value system, orientation, goals and life missions.

However, to us, success is not about being rich or famous, living in a mansion, having plenty of servants and bodyguards. The word success is having fun with what you do, enjoying the best of life, helping people in need and impacting the people around you of any age in a positive way.

Success also involves achieving your goals in life, fulfillment of your purpose and destiny by God.

How important would you say it is to be connected to other young people doing amazing things? How did you make these connections?

It is important to be connected to other young people doing amazing things because we can learn from each other, motivate, encourage and achieve more together. As we all know, there's strength in positive collaboration and this helps to make us motivated and focus on important tasks and projects. It is easy for us to connect with other young people doing great things around the world because of social media and organizations set up to support and encourage growing young entrepreneurs like us.

How important would you say reading and research is to the success of your business? What 3 business books would you recommend?

Reading and researching is an important aspect of entrepreneurship because from there, you learn more things and gain vital experience. We believe if you do the research and read books, you will become a successful young entrepreneur or change-maker. On our journey so far, we have come to know that there are lots of things that can be learned from reading and researching.

Some books we have read are ***Better Than a Lemonade Stand! Small Business Ideas for Kids*** by Daryl Bernstein, ***Starting your own business: Become an entrepreneur*** by Adam Toren and Matthew Toren, and ***The Toothpaste Millionaire*** by Jean Merrill.

If you could advise a future young mogul to do 3 things before starting their business what would they be?

It means a lot to us when it comes to giving advice to future change-makers because it's our mission to inspire young people to become young moguls like us. The three things we would tell young moguls before starting a business are:

1. To be passionate about what they are doing
2. Have a strategy on how to manage school, friends and fun with the business

3. Understand that it's a huge responsibility to own a business.

What are 3 lessons you have learned so far as a CEO, founder or public figure?
We have learned a of lot lessons so far on our journey as young entrepreneurs. However, the three major lessons we have learned so far as CEOs are:

- Patience - Creating and building a business takes time, effort and a whole lot of patience. Patience is a lesson that every entrepreneur will have to learn in order to build a successful business.
  This relates to the principle of sowing and reaping.
- Value for money - We have learned that rewards from business in terms of profit require hard work, consistency and diligence. This has made us understand that making money is not as easy as it seems. Therefore, we have learned to be prudent in our spending and to save more.
- Teachable spirits - A positive attitude and disposition to seek more knowledge daily and improve on your skills are extremely important in building up a successful business.

These lessons make us better people who are always improving on a daily basis, and as such can positively impact our business.

Where do you pull inspiration from?

We pull our inspiration from many things which include our environment, experiences, the works of our favorite chefs and bakers, and the ambition to be change-makers. Also, seeing other young entrepreneurs doing great things motivates us to continue. Lastly, getting recognized and appreciated also inspires us to do more.

What are 3 specific challenges you have had as a young mogul? How have you been able to overcome them?

We have had lots of challenges, but the following three were the most important:

- Publicity - Reaching out to people was a difficult task, because people did not take us seriously. This is because a lot of people did not and still do not believe in youth entrepreneurship.
  After a while, we noticed that social media was a key tool to be publicized, and this has been extremely helpful to our business.
- Defining our target market - At first, we just wanted to sell our products to people. Because we used premium ingredients, we struggled in selling because some people would say it's too expensive and some would buy. Consequently, we came to the realization that because we used premium ingredients, we could not be everyone's market and decide to target a specific market for our product and services, which has been extremely successful.
- Packaging - The presentation of our products was a key concern for our business because we wanted to have a great brand representation in the marketplace. This was a significant challenge at inception, but we have been able to overcome this successfully.

What are your goals for the future? What's next?

Our goals for the future are to continue to improve upon our skills and craft, seek opportunities, expand our business and collaborate with more young moguls to impact our world positively.

We are Culinary Connoisseurs and started our business at ages 10 & 7 years old. Our mission is to inspire and encourage children all over the world to dream BIG and follow their passion. In our business we help educate, stimulate and empower children and youths to follow their passion and to explore their creativity. We are also Ambassadors, Bloggers, Authors and Awardees. We hope to be able to work with you and help you carve a successful niche in life and impact your community.

ACKNOWLEDGEMENTS

A very special thank you to those who have supported my journey and helped me turn my dreams into a reality...

Olayinka O. Olaniyan; Olatayo Anidugbe Wusu; Mr. & Mrs. Michael O. Ogunyemi; Neil Wusu; Olufunke Ogunmodede; Augustine Gold; Ada Colon; Grandpa Deyo and Family Pastor Dupe Adefala; The Palm Waterfield School; Mary- Anne Aipoh- Ikoku; Delight Fusion Mr. Olajide Emmanuel Odeyemi; Mrs Olafunke Onofowora; Mrs Oluyemisi Adedotun; Mrs. Omobolanle Opuogen; Owonibi Timmy Samuel, Yetunde Akinyemi, Our American Aunties, Donald White

Chapter V. Polish & Profits
Positioning My Way to Success
Shaiann Hogan

www.shaisworld.com
Facebook.com/Shai'sWorld
Instagram.com/shaisworldshop
Twitter.com/shaisworldshop

Beauty is an outlet for creativity. A concept Shaiann Hogan understood from a young age. As a way to channel her individuality, Shaiann experimented with her mother's makeup and later filmed a makeup tutorial on her Itouch. Upon hearing the news, her mother wasn't too happy but it was at this moment, she saw passion and desire within her daughter. Qualities that are known to make a person even greater. Her mother began nurturing Shaiann's passion while providing her with the tools needed to propel. Soon, Shaiann learned to create her own custom nail polish and believed she could build an empire on something she loved. Months later, Shai's World was born.

Shai's World is an indie nail polish brand founded by Shaiann Hogan, a 14-year-old from Los Angeles, Calif. The business was launched in 2015 when Shaiann was only 10 years old. Shaiann wanted to create a fresh approach to the beauty industry by way of creating a vegan and cruelty-free nail polish. Shai's World is free from five harmful chemicals including formaldehyde, formaldehyde resins, toluene, dibutyl phthalate and camphor without sacrificing quality or performance. With a wide range of shades to choose from, Shaiann not only enjoys beauty but also tumbling, shopping and listening to music. Despite her busy "business" life, Shaiann is grounded in her academics with a competitive cumulative GPA.

Since launching her business, Shaiann has appeared on "The Real" talk show, "Harry TV" Show, Good Morning Washington, and has been featured in Teen Boss Magazine. Her accolades include receiving the NAACP Women in Spotlight Young Entrepreneur of the Year award in 2016, Placing second in the NFTE Urban League Biz Camp, and lastly receiving the "Her Eyes Matter" Black Business Women Rock 2017 award.

Shaiann is fueled with both goals and ambition. She reminds us all to sparkle and shine.

What is your favorite quote that can be printed on a T-shirt, written on a mirror or wall?

"Success consists of going from failure to failure with no loss of enthusiasm," by Winston Churchill

What are the 6 major ingredients or components that have contributed to the formulation of your success as a young changemaker thus far?

1. Prayer – I was born and raised in church with a strong background in religion. At the age of 4, I was a praise dancer. I danced for 8 years and even traveled while doing so. It was a way to express myself while in prayer. Although I don't dance as much today, I'm reminded by my parents and grandmother to always pray in everything I do. When challenges arise, I'm reminded to pray. Since being in business, it has allowed me to pray often as you will experience some highs and lows.
2. Great Product / Service – It's important to do the research on the product or service prior to starting business. Learn the industry, ask questions and put your own spin on it. Make sure the product / service is consistent, and your employees are well-trained. Creating a product and / or delivering a service takes lots of trial and error before placing on the market. Having a focus group is an ideal way to hear from potential customers about your product / service. It's a great way to connect with the customer as well.
3. Customer Service – Understanding your customers' wants and needs while bringing them an experience. Customer service is also rectifying an issue between you and the customer. I believe this is a huge factor in the life of business. Having quick problem-solving

43

skills to make the customer happy can help in the success of any business. To help with this, I have created lots of scenarios and solutions to help with customer service.

4. Partnering / Collaborations – My mom has her own business and has built lasting relationships since she's been in business more than 11 years, she has helped with the progression of my own business as I watch her lead by example. I have partnered with influencers, business owners and non-profits since being in business. It has helped with both sales and opportunities.

5. Building Relationships – I've learned quickly that relationships are the nucleus to growing a business. Authentic relationships allow for business opportunities. Each network is comprised of individuals who may know other individuals who can help grow the business. A business cannot grow without the help of others. It's a team effort, and once people learn to trust you, a relationship is formed. I never want my customer or wholesaler to feel that it's a one-time transaction and we're gone. I like to build the relationship so that it's a win-win for not only myself, but the other party as well. I like to create long term relationships that feel more like family.

6. Giving Back – This is necessary with any part of business. Whether it be your time, information or products. I have given to several organizations over the years. It not only helps others, but also brings about joy within myself when I'm able to help others.

What does your typical business or work day look like? When do you fit in fun, school, friends and family?

My typical business work day consists of waking up and checking emails to see if orders are in. If so, I pull inventory from my shelves to make the process faster and easier. However, if I need to restock nail polishes, I make them on Mondays and Wednesdays after school. I package and label products, print shipping labels and ship orders. My mom helps with marketing. I attend non-traditional school on Mondays and Wednesdays where I talk with my teacher and drop off work. If I need tutoring, I attend on Fridays. Saturdays are usually open for events or speaking engagements and if neither is on the calendar, I use it to hang with my friends at the mall or beach, only if there aren't any large orders in the pipeline. Sundays are usually family time. We attend church and grab a bite to eat afterward. Once we get home, we have a business meeting to discuss what's happening for the upcoming week. Afterwards, we have a little fun together.

What would you say success means to you? Why is it so important?

Success means to me being able to purposely live out my huge dream while accomplishing my goals and, in return, provide opportunities for others. It's important to me because I'm not only making myself happy, but inspiring and encouraging people from all walks of life. My business can help save a life, inspire a person, or even build confidence that they, too, can do it.

How important would you say it is to be connected to other young people doing amazing things? How did you make these connections?

It is very important to be connected to other young people doing amazing things as you are building your network. As we grow, our businesses grow. Furthermore, making the connections and collaborating with others will help to propel your business to newer heights. I've met lots of young people who are world-changers. Most are here within this book as well as online in a Facebook group named "Raising A Mogul Community." This community has allowed lots of connections to be made while encouraging and empowering each other. Imagine growing up and growing with each other while in business. My network will be powerful.

How important would you say reading and research is to the success of your business? What 3 business books would you recommended?

Reading is essential in the life of business. It's very important, and even more important when conducting research. Before starting my business, my mom and I read books, watched videos, took classes and joined nail polish groups. We saturated ourselves in understanding the world of beauty, in particular, nail polish. Even today, we are still learning and reading to get better. I enjoy John C. Maxwell books, especially these three:

How Successful People Think - teaching how to use effective thinking to capture success

How Successful People Lead - Mastering leadership skills to inspire and invest in people

How Successful People Win - The roadmap for winning even in adversity.

I enjoy John C. Maxwell books thoroughly. They are an easy read, with tools within to implement immediately into your life.

If you could advise a future young mogul to do 3 things before starting their business what would they be?

If I could advise a future young mogul to do three things before starting their business they would be: First, to definitely do your research. It sounds redundant, but it's by far the most important thing to do before starting any business. Learn the industry insides and outs. Google should be your best friend. Watch videos and ask questions. When I first decided to start my business, with the help of my mom, we purchased lots books. Some for business and others for the industry I was about to join. We also watched tons of videos from those we admired that had been in the industry for a while.

Next, find a mentor within your industry. Ask as many questions as possible while learning from them. They've made the mistakes already for you. Let them show you the way without making as many steps as they did. Utilize Facebook groups. Within most groups, you can learn a lot and also gain some knowledge about your industry that may help you in the future.

Lastly, make sure your paperwork is in order. Set up your business correctly, while taking pride in it. If you don't, what makes you think the world will? Choose your business structure and get the necessary insurance and permits needed to start your business. Set up your bank account while being sure to separate your personal from your business. Although we are young, we need to position ourselves to play big and do things professionally.

What are 3 lessons you have learned so far as a CEO, founder or public figure?

I have a learned a lot so far as a CEO/ founder of Shai's World. Three in particular, have been:

1. Stay Ready - As you grow, people will take notice of you and may have you do some things on the spot. This can include an interview, a picture and / or both. It is important for me to stay ready all the time. Opportunities come without notice. Carry business cards, dress appropriately and be ready to pitch at any given moment.

2. Stay Learning - Never stop learning from others. Especially from those whom you wish to be. Stay learning and ask questions.

3. Surround Yourself with Eagles - Surround yourself with people who elevate you. These are your cheerleaders and encouragers. They will blow wind beneath your wings so that you can soar high. They will push you and stretch you outside of your comfort zone.

Where do you pull inspiration from?

I pull inspiration from various places. My favorite is at the mall. Because I love to shop, seeing colors and stopping into beauty stores to see what's trending is not only fun, but helps me to stay "in the know" of what's happening in the beauty world. My nail tech, parents and grandmother also play roles in inspiring me. We have family nail parties with my nieces while having a mini focus group before I launch new collections. They can tell me what they like and don't like about the collection before deciding to launch.

What are 3 specific challenges you have had as a young mogul? How have you been able to overcome them?

My first biggest challenge was being able to learn time management. I'm a teenager and hanging out with my friends is fun, but so is making money selling my nail polish, and let's not forget having an extra-curricular activity is too! I had to learn how to balance them all while also going to school. It's hard. Even today, I still have this challenge. However, I use Google Calendar, which is helpful to plan out my weeks. Another challenge I have faced was a time when I had to pitch. I was unprepared as I did not have a cord for my laptop. It was a competition as well. Yikes! I had made it to round two. I was happy but couldn't really be in the moment as I did not have the proper tools to present on the screen projector. The judges were waiting patiently while I was in panic mode. Nevertheless, I was able to pull through and present after finding the cord needed and delivered. I placed second and was elated. However, I learned that being prepared is key. Since then, I'm making sure that I have everything I need prior. A lesson I will never forget. Lastly, another major challenge I have had has been separating my mom from mom-manager. It's difficult, as she wears both hats. Sometimes I'm confused and don't know which role she is playing. As time moves forward I'm getting better with learning and understanding the difference.

What are your goals for the future? What's next?

I plan to have purchase a house by the age of 20. I want to go to college and study to become a pediatric surgeon while running my nail polish business. Soon, I want to launch a vegan lip gloss line to compliment my nail polishes. It is also my goal to have my polishes in major retail locations and in several nail salons throughout the world. Lastly, as I grow, I want to hire teens like myself to help grow the business within different departments. This includes marketing, Social media, and some management positions.

I am the CEO of Shai's World and I started my business at 10 years old. My mission is to enhance the beauty of girls and women with vegan and cruelty-free nail polish. In my business, I help girls and women eliminate harmful chemicals from their nail polish without sacrificing quality or performance. I also am a high school student, a lover of all things beauty, a go-getter and a kidpreneur making an impact on the world. I hope to be able to work with you and help you to believe in the impossible.

ACKNOWLEDGEMENTS

A very special thank you to those who have supported my journey and helped me turn my dreams into a reality...

Mom Toushonta Hoga; Dad Kevin Hogan; Nanny Rochelle Davis; Chasity Miller-Bell; Anastacia, D'Omdrae Landers; Uri Dawson; Candance Simmons; Uncle Charles Berry; Margaret Thomas-Gite; Papa Gervis Grimble; Danielle Holloway; Cherise Dwyer; Betty Porter; Myisha Koonce; Uncle James Massengale; Godmommy Denise Williams; Nuvia Castro; Natasha White; Uncle Willie.

Chapter VI. Creating Success Through Tragedy
Kennedi Harris

www.klockproducts.com
Facebook.com/klockproduct
Instagram.com/klock_products

Kennedi Harris is 8 years old, she was born and raised in Stone Mountain, Ga. Kennedi had a traumatic experience at the beginning of a school year, whereby she was taken by mistake out of her school district and taken to another county to the Department of Children and Family Services. In order to cope with the traumatic experience, we started a fun business for Kennedi which turned into a very successful business that has spread nationally and internationally with customers. K-lock is an identification locket custom designed and personalized to prevent misidentification of children in schools and daycare. Starting her own business took her mind away from things as she enjoyed adding a personal touch to each product. K-lock also has African American dolls that are now available. She created the lockets to properly identify kids in school in daycares and on field trips. She also has signature T-shirts, hats, lip balm and lotions. Kennedi has been featured in several magazines, including *Teen Boss Magazine*, *KidNewsMaker* Magazine and *My Time* magazine. Kennedi is an honor roll student and just recently conducted career day at her school featuring her business rather than her parents explaining their careers. Kennedi's mission with her business is to ensure that no other child is misidentified in the school system, or in any other similar environment. Her aim is also to show other kids a role model which they can look to for leadership, and how to start a business of their own. She hopes that her business model will give other kids her age an example and a blueprint to show that they, too, can do anything in life and create their own businesses. Kennedi enjoys education, especially financial literacy. She feels that it is important for her to know grown-up information to run her business. Kennedi understands the importance of her influence with other people by speaking to them about success in general and having a "you can do it" attitude.

What is your favorite quote that can be printed on a T-shirt, written on a mirror or wall?

My favorite quote that can be printed on a T-shirt, written on a mirror or wall is "Be true to yourself, never give up and persevere." For anyone who might go through what I had to go through, they may want to give up. This is why I feel it is very important that no matter what bad things happened to you that you keep moving forward to reach your goals. I think that you should always do the things that are important to you and not worry about what others think you should do.

What are the 6 major ingredients or components that have contributed to the formulation of your success as a young change-maker thus far?

The six major ingredients or components that have contributed to the formulation of my success as a young change-maker thus far are staying focused, having a great dad and family to help me, listening to business books on audio, seeing and understanding the value of money and understanding that business isn't always easy. It helps balance between being a kid and business owner. my dad and I have always had a super special bond that cannot be broken. He is always there for me and makes me feel safe. He is always encouraging me to do my best and to be my best. My brother and stepmom are always there to support everything that I do. My step-mom always encourages me and we do a lot of cool things together. My brother and I always have a lot of fun and he supports my business. I read my parents books and listen to their audios when we are in the car. They help me to understand how to run my company and understand money.

What does your typical business or work day look like? When do you fit in fun, school, friends and family?

My typical business day usually goes in this order: school, homework, business. The business task may include packing and shipping. my parents taught me the importance of properly packaging my products. When I'm done with my business task, then it's time for fun. I have a lot of fun on weekends and just before bed. I like watching movies and traveling. Some of my favorite places are Jamaica, Bahamas and Costa Rica. A full business day may include packing for events at home, a vendor event on a Saturday morning for a few hours, then after I have gotten home after the event we do inventory. That's when we count up money and products. That's my favorite part.

What would you say success means to you? Why is it so important?

Success to me means having savings for the future. It's important to me so that I can purchase my own house before I'm 20 years old. I think it is important for me to build my business, because it helps other kids know that they can do it also. My dad always tells me that it is important to serve other people in my company and I will always be rewarded.

(What does it mean to purchase your house when you're 20 years old?)

I'll be the first to purchase a house before the age of 20 in my family. I think this is important because it shows that kids can do adult business deals. It also gives me a chance to help people have a place to live. By doing this it also allows me to be able to have money for college and to put some back into my business to make it grow.

How important would you say it is to be connected to other young people doing amazing things? How did you make these connections?

It is important to be connected to other young people doing amazing things because my friends don't understand the life of a business owner plus being a kid. My friends who don't have businesses don't understand that I can't make it to a birthday party sometimes because I have an event or interview. I made these connections by meeting friends at kids' business fairs. My parents always teach me that when I do things that other people are not willing to do, I will be able to have, do, and live like they won't be able to do. They teach me that it is important to be around other people who think like me. My dad teaches me that if I hang around people who are not positive it will make me behave in a negative way. I also feel that I make people grow their businesses to be successful when they see me be successful.

How important would you say reading and research is to the success of your business? What 3 business books would you recommend?

I would say reading and research is important to the success of my business so that I can learn more about business. it is important to research my business so that I can explain why I do certain things in my business. It is important to know the answers to your business when people ask you. it is always important to read so that you learn new things to make your business better. I will recommend my daddy's book *Leaning Forward Toward Success*, *Raising a Kidpreneur* by my dad and I, and *Queen of The Court* by Serena Williams. She's my favorite athlete. Her whole story is awesome. I like Serena so much because she always fights hard to win and be her best. In her book she has many stories telling how she made it to the top. She is a huge inspiration for anybody in business and in everyday life.

If you could advise a future young mogul to do 3 things before starting their business what would that be?

If I could advise a future young mogul to do three things before starting their business, it would be to do research on your product before going to your parents, save your money and be willing to give up some fun time. it is important to research your business to know if it will be a business that people want need and will continue to support. It is important to save your money so that you can have the money needed to buy products and material for your company. My dad always explains to me that my time is very important and that I have to give some of my time to grow my business so that I will have a lot of time to myself later because of my Success.

What are 3 lessons you have learned so far as a CEO, founder or public figure?

The three lessons that I have learned so far as a CEO is, some of the money that you earn you have to put back into your business. I learned that I cannot grow my business if I do not reinvest back into my business. My parents always teach me that you cannot eat all of your seed money that you have to put some back in your business to make it grow. Also how to manage my time. My dad always says that you can't get back time so I must use it wisely. I have to do the important things first and use what time is left over to do the smaller things that are not as important. Also, that it takes hard work to be a business owner. My parents teach me that making my business grow will not always be easy. There will be times where I may not go to play with my friends because I have to attend an event to sell my products. There are sometimes where I may have to get up really early or stay up really late because we have a vending event. These are the things that are required to have a successful business.

Where do you pull inspiration from? Person, place or thing

I pull inspiration from my daddy. I always want him to be proud of me. My step mom and my brother also inspire me and make me want to always do my best.

What are 3 specific challenges you have had as a young mogul? How have you been able to overcome them?

Three specific challenges I have had as a young mogul are talking to big crowds. I'm still overcoming that but practicing in front of small crowds is helping. Trusting people after my incident of being misidentified is another one. I overcame that by talking to people at my events, sharing my business and products with as many people as possible. The third challenge is realizing that I can have a kid business in an adult world. I overcame that by seeing that I can make as much money as an adult.

What are your goals for the future? What's next?

My goals for the future and what's next are to grow my business and add more products. I want to always have products and services that people want need and will buy again. I want my products to make people happy. I want to be in more magazines and on more TV shows so that I can share my story with the world. I am beginning my speaking career and I am excited to be able to travel around the world sharing my story and inspiring others.

I am a Kennedi Harris, K-lock CEO, and I started my business at 7 years old. My mission is to positively affect people through my experience of being misidentified. In my business I help schools, daycares and business owners to prevent misidentification of kids. I'm also an author, speaker, honor roll student and leader. I hope to be able to work with you and help to empower you to achieve your dreams and believe in yourself.

Chapter VII. The Joy in Purpose
Joy Alexis Paulk

www.thejoycornerbnb.com
Facebook.com/TheJoyCorner
Instagram.com/TheJoyCorner_BnB
Twitter.com/TheJoyCornerBnB
Linkedin.com/in/TheJoyCornerBnB.com

Joy Alexis Paulk (born November 15, 1998) was raised in Southern California. She graduated from Paul Mitchell The School and is currently in college for music therapy.

Joy is the CEO and founder of The Joy Corner Beauty and Beyond, as well as the co-founder of Destiny Joy Inc. She has dedicated years of diligence to the family business. As a result, she has maintained a consistent presence among the children and families in foster care. Joy desires to combat the epidemic of bullying, the mentality of being nugatory and suicidal gestures. By embracing her passion, she guides youth toward the pursuit of self-worth and joy. Along with her inspirational performances at special events, Joy has added The Joy Corner Beauty and Beyond. This is where she does girls' hair, makeup and nails at no cost. A special bonus is her boutique, which completes and enhances the clients' beauty experience from the inside out.

Joy discovered that giving a word of encouragement and sharing your story or talent(s) is indispensable. These gestures go a long way in the life of someone in need. She also includes testimonies and inspirational workshops in her encounter with the girls. Joy's efforts have shown her determination to take her empowering business on the road. She is working toward a mobile salon so that she can go to those in need. Joy is currently in the studio recording inspirational songs to revitalize her peers abroad.

The second phase of Joy's master plan is to create a hospitable and rejuvenating atmosphere for those who are demoralized, to introduce them to a life of momentum, exhibit their ardor and stimulate productivity. The state-of-the-art therapeutic center will be comprised of creative art therapy, inspirational workshops, music, theatre, career development, the beauty salon and boutique. Joy looks forward to manifesting her message of influence, impacting the lives of these very special children, and rising to national platforms.

Joy states that, "I cannot imagine having the opportunity to impact a life and not making every effort to do so." She is honored to be the vessel, to bridge the gap between loving and broken souls. Joy's message to the world is:

"Your life is validated. Your life does not end with your past tribulations, let your adversity catapult you to your destiny and turn your broken pieces into masterpieces."

What is your favorite quote that can be printed on a T-shirt, written on a mirror or wall?

My number one favorite quote is, "Aspire to inspire." I've always had the desire to help and inspire the people around me. I feel like others should aspire to do so, too.

What are the 6 major ingredients or components that have contributed to the formulation of your success as a young change-maker thus far?

I learned a very valuable lesson early on: If I wanted to be successful, I needed to love what I was doing. I needed to know why I was doing it, and I needed to believe in myself. So, I began my journey to seek my purpose.

I begin my day by reading a passage or verse in the Bible and praying. Why? I believe that I was designed by God with a purpose for a purpose. My purpose is to use my gifts and talents to make a difference in the lives of others. If I want to know what my purpose is, and how to best use the tools that were given to me, I need to go straight to the source. For instance, if I want instruction to operate a new TV, I look at its manual. God provides the blueprint, design and roadmap for my life, and I want to make sure that I'm on the right path to my destiny. Jeremiah 29:11 says, "For I know the plans I have for you," declares the Lord. "Plans for you to prosper and not harm; Plans to give you hope and a future." His plans are always working for my good and the good of the world. He has the best plan for my life.

Knowing my purpose has generated the passion and the fuel necessary to motivate me every day. I wake up in the morning with great expectation and excitement because I understand that I was blessed with another day, and I don't take that for granted. I understand that each new day has a purpose, and I have the honor to impact another life.

It is not enough to just read and pray, I must see it, speak it, and do it! If I want to be an inspiration to other young people, I must first be inspired. (Proverbs 18:21) "Life and death are in the power of my tongue," I speak positive declarations while looking in the mirror; I declare. I am fearfully and wonderfully made, I am more than a conqueror, I am smart, I'm beautiful, I'm valuable, I will overcome every adversity that comes my way. I will never give up! Speaking positive words daily equips me to speak life into myself and others. I set out to be the solution to the problem that is close to my heart, so it is important that I am equipped. Putting the oxygen mask on myself first is an important ingredient.

Doing what I love while perfecting my gifts and talents. Being committed to cultivating my various means to reach the youth is a very important component. I believe my purpose in life goes beyond my own satisfaction and has a larger place in this world, so I have a responsibility to be the best that I can be. This life is not just about me. In these times where bullying is running rampant and suicide is on the rise, I am compelled to do what I can to help as many youths as possible to find their worth and to fight for their lives. I found that my purpose in life is to inspire and encourage the youth through the gifts that God has placed in my life, which is through music, dance, cosmetology, fashion, health, and fitness. The best way to execute my purpose is to perfect my gifts and talents by putting in hours of practice, time, and development.

To be self-disciplined and tenacious. God gave me this assignment, and nobody is going to care about the success of the outcome of my purpose and destiny more than me. I made up my mind that it is not an option for me to give up. I believe in myself, but I have to put in the work to accomplish my goal. People will come and go in my life and people have their own purpose to live out. It is my responsibility to motivate myself. I wake up early, meditate, plan my day, eat a healthy breakfast and exercise before school and work. Having a disciplined routine allows me to maintain my physical and mental well-being. It also sustains my clarity, focus and stamina throughout the day. Doing these things contribute to making a more productive day. When you have tenacity, it allows you to withhold the strength and courage to overcome hardship, mental battles, and difficulty in your life. Discipline and tenacity is determination in action.

To have a joyful heart because it is contagious. I work with girls, many of whom have experienced trauma, and it is important for me to have a joyful heart because it is contagious. Joyfulness builds a positive community around you and it creates an atmosphere conducive to healing and restoration. Nehemiah 8:10 in the Bible says, "The joy of the Lord is my strength".

Research and having knowledge. Having further knowledge allows me to be as equipped as I possibly can to better serve the youth that I work with. It is imperative that I understand their plight to be able to successfully contribute to their lives.

Connecting with the community and having fun. Networking is a valuable tool and one of the most essential aspects of building my business. Developing relationships and connecting with others has given me many opportunities to advance my business by strengthening my referral base. Volunteering is also a great way to broaden the network. Serving and helping others, helps me to build the community around me. Everyone wins!

What does your typical business or work day look like? When do you fit in fun, school, friends and family?
A typical work day for me starts with prayer and devotions. That also can be a time to reflect on what I did prior to that day and see how I can improve and work on for the present day. Next, I write a to-do list so that I can get a clear perspective of my day. That also includes checking emails, messages, social media outlets and my calendar. I make sure I use a couple hours of the day to rehearse for any upcoming events and just to further my skills in music. As a full-time college student, school is also a major part of my work day. Studying and practicing prepare me to go into music therapy. If I have a client to do hair or makeup for, or have a workshop with the youth for that day, I will make sure I have all

my tools and supplies together. Once I have completed the most important things on my to-do list, I make sure I have time to do fun things with my friends and family because balance is very important.

What would you say success means to you? Why is it so important?

Fulfilling my purpose with excellence and passion, peace and joy. I work with youth who have been abused, neglected and abandoned, and I also work with people who have all the money and possessions in the world. One thing that I have learned is that hopelessness comes in all forms. So, when I think of success, it must come from a deeper place than what is on the surface. When I think of success, I think of longevity finishing the course of my purpose. I think of doing the seemingly impossible and when all heck breaks loose in life, I will still rise and shine. I think of my purpose.

In my life, I have witnessed bullying, harassment and tearing down of my peers. I have seen my peers suffering from suicidal ideations, suicide attempts, suicide, and there is no prejudice in its racial or economic status. There is a misconception that if someone has a lot of money, big houses, fancy cars and can travel the world, that they live with absolutely no problems and that's success. There are the countless cases in which people who are on top have committed suicide or have drowned their negative thoughts with drugs, alcohol and promiscuous behavior to cover the pain.

What has become clear to me is having trust in God and confidence that no matter what happens in my life, He is going to work it out for my good. So, having peace that surpasses all understanding will guard my heart and mind. Knowing that in this life, there will be heartache, failures, disappointment and pain, more than material and monetary success, is necessary.

Having joy in my life is vital. When I'm worn out from things not going my way or experiencing disappointment, I have joy in my heart that is not contingent on what is happening around me. Possessing the presence of hope and always having the feeling of excitement make everyday a success. I have expectation of filling my goals and plans, fully embracing and enjoying the journey. Success to me is knowing that I have already inspired, encouraged, and empowered thousands of young girls and brought joy in their lives, and I will continue to do so.

I truly believe that people don't remember you for what you've done, but for how you've made them feel. There is no greater feeling for

58

me than knowing I have touched and made a difference in someone's life. To me, success looks like being the absolute best version of myself. Success defined is the accomplishment of a purpose. Yes, it can also mean the attainment of wealth and popularity, but there is something about having a divine purpose behind what you do. My success is important because other lives depend on it.

I'm so very excited about phase one of my next level of serving the young ladies in group homes. Many of the girls that I work with have never been to a professional salon, and they often have transportation challenges. It will be my pleasure to take my service to them by way of a mobile salon. Doing the girls' hair and makeup for their special occasions has brought me so much joy. Making them feel beautiful and special on days that many of us take for granted is priceless. When I think of success, I think of the smiles that the girls have on their faces when they look in the mirror. I think about how grateful they always are because I took the time out of my work schedule to make them feel special on their important day. And I must say that there has never been a time in all my years of serving the youth that they didn't bless me right back. I often think about this beautiful young girl who said, "I want to be just like Joy," or those young ladies who say I inspired them to follow their dreams and work hard so they can bless young girls the way I have blessed them. This is what success looks like to me.

How important would you say it is to be connected to other young people doing amazing things? How did you make these connections?

It's extremely important to be connected with other young individuals because we can inspire one another. We can help sharpen our knowledge and skills, so we can all be more effective in the world. We can never have enough successful and encouraging people. It is never a competition, but an amazing contribution to many others who need positivity in their lives. Building strong relationships with other like-minded individuals will strengthen insight and can only help us to be better in everything that we do. Together, we can make this world a better place. I have made many of my powerful connections at business expos, church youth events, school leadership clubs and college.

How important would you say reading and research is to the success of your business? What 3 business books would you recommend?

Reading and researching your business will help guide an idea of your startup, into a reality. From the moment an idea is sparked about starting your own business, start researching.

A couple of things that you can start researching are:

1.   What your product or service will be
2.   Your target market
3.   How can you reach your customers
4.   Similar businesses

Putting in the time in researching and reading about your business will increase your knowledge and progress, whether you are just starting or have already been in the game. The more knowledge you obtain the more you can pour into your business and others. It is really difficult for me to narrow it down to three books, but I thought it was very important for me to really have a strong foundation for my purpose and career in life. I was inspired by great authors such as Joyce Meyers, T.D. Jakes and Steve Harvey. These three books also spoke to my heart:

1. *My Child is Going to be Rich & Famous* by Angela J. William
2. ***The Purpose Driven Life*** by Rick Warren
3. ***The Hollywood Commandments: A Spiritual Guide to Secular Success*** by Devon Franklin

If you could advise a future young mogul to do 3 things before starting their business what would they be?

Number one, know and understand your purpose. Number two, be daring and follow your heart. Number three, be determined and never give up.

What are 3 lessons you have learned so far as a CEO, founder or public figure?

Number one, that I always must be a self-starter and self-motivating. Number two, I must have great organizational skills. And number three, I have to make sacrifices and work very hard if I want to succeed.

Where do you pull inspiration from?

I pull my inspiration from God, my ultimate encourager, my parents, Martin and Desiree Paulk, my role models, my sisters, Noel

O'Mara and Destiny Paulk, who were always there for me, and the girls that I work with. I am such a combination of my mom and dad. I watch them pour heart, time and resources into the lives of children, youth and families in foster care and people in general, all my life. I grew up with the passion to help others as well. I also share my love for the arts, singing and music with from father, and helping youth, business and dance, from my mother. I love it all, and I'm so very thankful that I can use it all. I am also inspired by the girls I work with because the more I see the need to speak life into the lives of someone, the more I'm inspired to do so.

What are 3 specific challenges you have had as a young mogul? How have you been able to overcome them?

1. Balancing school, work and extra activities.
2. Organizing all the various tasks.
3. Staying focused on the most important things.

Having great organizational skills is a challenge I am still working toward mastering. Being able to be organized is a very important factor, not only for business, but for your day-to-day life. Entering college was a huge challenge for me: the school work, studying and staying up all night was all quite new. On top of being in college, I have to balance work, practicing, and fitting in free time. Time management is a continuous challenge that many people struggle with, even I am still trying to find ways to stay on track so day by day I can accomplish as much as I can. Twenty-four hours in a day could go by in a blink of an eye, sometimes I even ask myself how I can complete each task that needs to be done. I found that planning out my day ahead of time, writing a to-do list and making sure I am devoting each hour of the day to the important things first before I relax has played a major role in overcoming this challenge. At this age, focusing on the important things that need to be done can be very challenging. It's OK to have fun and to give yourself free time, however, concentrating on your goals in life now could steer you in the right direction to a successful future. Remember that you are never too young to start working toward your dream.

What are your goals for the future? What's next?

I am working on having my very own creative art therapeutic center. This center will be a beautiful ranch style location designed to give the youth an experience that they may have never had. From the time they walk in it will be visually beautiful, with an atmosphere of serenity to allow the kids to let their guard down. I want them to be relaxed and open to receive everything our programs have to offer. The center will have a multitude of creative art therapy including dance, music, various types of productions, a recording studio and more. My plans are to record inspirational songs that will inspire the youth to fight for their lives, dreams, and to never give up! We will have programs to prepare them for their careers, life skills, personal development, and health and fitness programs. The center will offer complete physical health, mental health and social well-being programs. Being able to use the combination of the things that I love to make a difference in the lives of others is what success looks like to me. I look forward to impacting millions.

I am Joy Alexis Paulk, founder and CEO of Destiny Joy Inc. (non-profit) and The Joy Corner Beauty and Beyond (salon and boutique). I started my journey serving youth in foster care when I was 14 years old. My mission is to inspire dreams, empower purpose, nurture passion and foster hope for at-risk youth, youth in foster care and youth with special needs. I aim to combat the growing epidemic of suicide and hopelessness caused by mental health issues, trauma, abuse and bullying. I am a singer, dancer, cosmetologist, motivator and college student studying music therapy. I hope to work with you and help you by joining together, using our gifts and talents to educate youth, prepare them for success, be a beacon of bright light and to bring joy to this world.

ACKNOWLEDGEMENTS

A very special thank you to those who have supported my journey and helped me turn my dreams into a reality...

Mark & Tracey Paulk; Margie Pizarre; Christel Richards; RJ Jackson; Kim Hillman; Shawn LaRe Brinkley; Marlene Williams; Darian Davis Jr.; Ernesa Ramdeen; Marlo Stroud; Kenya Myer; Blaise Brooks; Varant Marjarian; Kathy Grant; Carla Carr; Marcia Tinoco; Shawn Lynn Adams; Kelley Medley; Arianna Williams

Chapter VIII. Dream BIG and Work HARD
Desiayah Dean

www.sciencewithdesiayah.com
Facebook.com/sciencewithdesiayah
Instagram.com/sciencewithdesiayah

Desiayah Dean is a 10-year-old, fun-loving author and entrepreneur from Newport News, Va. She loves reading, writing, soccer, football and playing with her little brother, Jacory. Desiayah is the owner of Science with Desiayah, established in 2016 and created from her love of science and desire to show kids around the world how fun science can be. Her business started when she began selling slime at school, and now she creates fun science kits with some of her favorite experiments. She also enjoys teaching science and slime workshops. After selling out at the Richmond Children's Business Fair, she had the opportunity to be a part of a commercial campaign with CW Richmond and Bounce TV that highlighted young entrepreneurs. Desiayah believes with hard work, faith and creativity all things are possible. She wants children everywhere to believe they can do anything they put their minds to. There have been ups and downs in her entrepreneurial journey, but Desiayah believes it has all been worth it. Science with Desiayah retails online and at local events.

What is your favorite quote that can be printed on a T-shirt, written on a mirror or wall?

My favorite quote is "Why fit in when you are born to stand out?" by Dr. Seuss. I like this quote because we are all created differently, so why not show it and be proud of it? I don't want to be like someone else. We should all be happy that we're unique.

What are the 6 major ingredients or components that have contributed to the formulation of your success as a young change-maker thus far?

The first ingredient that has contributed to the formulation of my success is hard work, because without hard work, I wouldn't get anything done. Hard work for me is sometimes staying up late, testing out my recipes and experiments to make sure they are right and shipping orders. Number two is the family support I have, because everyone needs help. I can't do everything all on my own. My family is always there to help by taking me to different events, investing and encouraging me. Number three is discipline, because it keeps me focused on my goals. Four is sacrifice. Sometimes I have to miss out on some things in order to get work done. I have to sacrifice soccer games or going outside to play to attend business events. Five is commitment. I have to tell myself all the time I will finish this, and I will never give up. And the sixth ingredient is fun. Have fun and love what you do.

What does your typical business or work day look like? When do you fit in fun, school, friends and family?

I'm homeschooled, so when I wake up, I eat breakfast and get dressed. After that, I start on my schoolwork. After my work is done, I take a break, and if I have anything to do for my business, I will work on it then. I write my goals down and a to-do list, so I know what I have to work on for my business each day. Some days I will have PE class or soccer practice. If I have soccer practice, or a soccer game, I go there. But if I don't, I will go outside and play with my friends.

What would you say success means to you? Why is it so important?

Success to me means having family and friends you can count on. It's important to me because I know they will always be there for me. It also means achieving my goals, which is important because it proves to myself that I can do anything.

How important would you say it is to be connected to other young people doing amazing things? How did you make these connections?

It's very important to stay connected with other young people who are doing similar things because it helps me to stay motivated and set bigger goals for myself. I meet different kids at business events and through social media. We exchange business cards, invite each other to events and congratulate each other on our successes.

How important would you say reading and research is to the success of your business? What 3 business books would you recommend?

Reading and research is very important because you have to learn about business and what you want to do. If you don't learn, you won't grow. The first book I would recommend is *Young Entrepreneurs with Big Ideas* by Adam and Matthew Toren. This is the first book I read which taught me what an entrepreneur was and ways to become one. Another good book is *Better than a Lemonade Stand: Small Business Ideas for Kids* by Daryl Bernstein. This book also talks about business basics and it gives a lot of cool business ideas for kids. And the last book would be *How to turn $100 into $1,000,000: Earn! Save! Invest!* by James McKenna and Jeannine Glista, which is all about saving and investing your money.

If you could advise a future young mogul to do 3 things before starting their business what would they be?

The three things I would advise a future young mogul to do would be: First, think about what you would like to do and talk to your family about it. When I decided to sell slime, I told my mom and asked if she could help me with buying supplies. Next, do your research. Find classes, videos or books about your topic so you can learn as much as possible. I watched a lot of videos to learn how to make the perfect slime. After a lot of trial and error, I found what worked best for me and also wrote my first book 7 *Secrets to Making the Perfect Slime*. The last thing would be GET STARTED, no matter how big or small. Just GET STARTED.

What are 3 lessons you've learned so far as a CEO, founder or public figure?
The first lesson I learned is that everything doesn't always work out. Sometimes you make money, sometimes you lose money. Sometimes an idea you have doesn't work, and sometimes it does. The second lesson is that you must believe in yourself and never give up no matter how hard it gets. Sometimes I take a break to get myself together, but I

always come back and finish. The last lesson is that hard work really does pay off. When I look at everything I've done, I'm so proud of myself.

Where do you pull inspiration from?
I pull inspiration from other businesses, my mom, my dad and my grandmothers. I also pull inspiration and ideas from going to different business events. My mom owns a business doing hair. Watching her encourages me to never give up. My dad teaches me to always work hard and my grandmothers are always there supporting me. They all help me to grow and learn and that helps me to grow my business bigger and bigger.

What are 3 specific challenges you have had as a young mogul? How have you been able to overcome them?
My biggest challenge has been trial and error. When making my science kits, some experiments fail and were a disaster. And it took time just to get the right containers and packaging for everything. I overcame this by never giving up, and I just kept trying until I got it right. Time management was also a challenge at the beginning. I have had to learn to discipline myself and not wait until the last minute to complete things. I have also had to learn how to be more comfortable speaking at events. The more I do it, the easier it gets. I pretend that the room is empty or I just look at my mom and pretend we are having a conversation.

What are your goals for the future? What's next?
I plan to continue creating awesome science kits and selling them all over the world. I want everyone to know how fun science is. I also love baking and I want to start my own baking business one day. I want to start taking classes to improve my baking skills.

I am an author and entrepreneur, and I started my business at 8 years old. My mission is to teach boys and girls all over the world that science is fun. In my business, I help kids to enjoy science by creating fun, easy-to-do science kits. I am also a very creative, loving, funny and helpful person. I hope to be able to work with you and help you enjoy science as much as I do.

ACKNOWLEDGEMENTS

A very special thank you to those who have supported my journey and helped me turn my dreams into a reality...

Harold Dean; Rossie Dean; Jacory Dean; Linda Jones; Mildred Dean; Mildred Byrd; Ryan Taylor; Tier-ra Henry; Gail Taylor; Angela Tisdale; Allison Moore; Tracie Judd; Saidea Kromah; Janet Landwehr; Caroline Benedum; Caelyn Driscoll; Appreleia Bullock; Jay Cameron; Candice James-Walker

Chapter IX. Caking It to Disney World!
Ziggy and Tootie

www.ziggyandtootie.com
Facebook.com/ziggyandtootie
Instagram.com/ziggyandtootie
Twitter.com/ziggyandtootie

Ziggy and Tootie are two young moguls who are mastering the art of entrepreneurship in the 21st century. At only 6 and 7 years old, these two young moguls are junior pastry chefs, junior professors, social media influencers, and authors. They are the CEOs and founders of Ziggy and Tootie Cakes, and the Ziggy and Tootie LLC.

These young ladies are sisters and the daughters of retired Air Force veterans, Alphonso Quinn and Dr. Sheva Quinn. Although they were born on Lakenheath Royal Air Force Base, England, they are living their lives to the fullest in Byron, Georgia, with their parents.

The girls started their entrepreneurship journey as a micro-home-based business at the tender ages of 3 and 4 as junior pastry chefs. With a $500 investment from their mother, they used Facebook advertisements to secure profits on their first bake sale. In 2017, the girls used their commission to fund a first-class vacation to Disney World! Ziggy and Tootie are an international brand with recurring customers in the United Kingdom, Africa, Korea and Japan.

In 2017, Ziggy and Tootie decided to expand their brand into public broadcasting by way of a YouTube channel, titled "Ziggy and Tootie". In less than two months on YouTube, they signed their first endorsement deal and became social media influencers. Every Friday evening, the girls go live on YouTube to promote their favorite kid-friendly books or products.

Ziggy and Tootie have been featured on NBC News, PBS New Hour, the Regina Sunshine Robinson Show, Museum of Aviation and local news stations. They are the go-to youth for local endorsement and community advertisement.

Both girls are homeschooled and entrepreneurship is part of their curriculum. They are also active members of the Girl Scout organization and the Jr. First Lego League robotics teams. In the fall of 2018, they plan to expand their business into a line of custom-designed cookies. Their primary mission in life is to gain as much wisdom and knowledge as possible so that they can continue to make all their dreams come true!

What is your favorite quote that can be printed on a T-shirt, written on a mirror or wall?

Our favorite quote that can be printed on a T-shirt, is our personal quote, "Bake the Cake!"

What are the 6 major ingredients or components that have contributed to the formulation of your success as a young change-maker thus far?

The six major ingredients that have contributed to our success are:

1. Our mom's support
2. Focus and dedication to the business of cakes
3. Preparation through reading and research
4. Experimenting with different and new recipes
5. Social media
6. Networking with other young CEOs

What does your typical business or work day look like? When do you fit in fun, school, friends and family?

Because we are homeschooled, a typical business day is not much different from any other day. We are continuously learning about business and entrepreneurship as part of our curriculum. We have entrepreneurship and business classes two days a week, and we work in our business on weekends, holidays, and over the summer. On the weekends that we are not working, we hang out with our family and friends and do lots of fun things such as going to water and amusement parks. Our family has a big Sunday dinner with grandparents, aunts, uncles, cousins and friends once a month, so we get to spend time and catch up with our extended family then. We also take a big family vacation to Disney World at the end of each year.

What would you say success means to you? Why is it so important?

To us, success is earning enough money throughout the year so that we can have a great vacation at Disney World. Having a fun and exciting vacation at Disney World is important to us because it is our most favorite place in the world! And we believe that after a long year of work in both school and in business, we should have a great vacation!

How important would you say it is to be connected to other young people doing amazing things? How did you make these connections?

We think that being connected to other young people in business is very important because although being a kid entrepreneur is hard work, it is also very fun and exciting. We think that it is great to be able to talk with other kids that have amazing businesses, and to have someone to discuss new business ideas and concepts with.

One way we connect with other kids is through teaching in our business school, the *Young CEO Academy*. Our school is on our website at www.ziggyandtootie.com. We also are members of social media groups that were created for kids in business and their parents. And we attend vending and networking events that are designed for kid entrepreneurs.

How important would you say reading and research is to the success of your business? What 3 business books would you recommend?

We believe that reading books and researching our business is very important and necessary for our business success. Through reading and researching, we learn new cake recipes and how to make better business decisions.

The first kid-friendly entrepreneur book that our mom ever bought us that we highly recommend is *What Does It Mean to Be an Entrepreneur?* by Rana DiOrio and Emma D. Dryden. The second book we recommend and the book our mom used to teach us about the history of wealth and entrepreneurship is *Mansa Musa: The Lion of Mali* by Khephra Burns. The third book we enjoy reading and recommend to anyone that is starting a cake business is *The Cupcake Diaries* by Katherine Kallinis and Sophia Kallinis LaMontagne. It is about two sisters that have a cupcake business together, the same as we do!

If you could advise a future young mogul to do 3 things before starting their business, what would they be?

If we could advise future young moguls on three things in starting a business, we would advise:

1. First, select a business name and research the name that you selected to make sure no one else in your state has the same business name.
2. Make sure you have great packaging and delivery of your product or service.
3. Take lots of notes to improve your marketing and advertising.

What are 3 lessons you have learned so far as a CEO, founder or public figure?

As CEOs, we have learned that having our mom's support is very important to the success of our business. Although we make all the final decisions about our business, our mom makes sure that they are carried through. We have also learned that we must have a plan and a strategy for success. We make the most money in our business when we has a solid plan and strategy. Finally, we have learned that it is OK to make mistakes in business, you just have to recover well.

Where do you pull inspiration from?

Without a doubt, we pull our inspiration from our Mommy! Our mom is patient with us, and she lets us experiment in the kitchen, even with new groceries! She gets up early to manage our business while we are still sleeping, and she takes us to new and fun places to sell our cakes. Our mom makes business fun!

What are 3 specific challenges you have had as a young mogul? How have you been able to overcome them?

In having a cake business, we have had many challenges. One challenge that we had early in our business is having too many cakes at vending events. Therefore, we came up with a strategy that enabled us to carry less cakes and still secure our profit goal. Another challenge we had was with recipes. We thought that if we used a recipe from the Internet that it would turn out great. We quickly learned that Internet recipes do not work well. We overcame the challenge by sending our mom to pastry school. In school, she learned how to develop a cake recipe that works well for our business model. Our third challenge has been sharing kitchen space. We overcame the shared kitchen space challenge by having our mommy make crockpot meals and use disposable dishes on baking days. That way there is less cooking and dishwashing that we have to do.

What are your goals for the future? What's next?

The next business goal for Ziggy and Tootie Cakes is making customized cookies!

We are Ziggy and Tootie, founders and CEOs of Ziggy and Tootie Cakes, and Ziggy and Tootie LLC. We started our business when we were 3 and 4 years old. Our mission is to raise money for great vacations to Disney World! We satisfy people's sweet tooth with our delicious southern classic cakes. Our customers are people young and old who love cake! In our business, we solved the challenge of delivering a taste of home to the men and women serving overseas in the United States Armed Forces. We are also junior professors, authors and social media influencers. We hope to be able to work with you, and to help you become a cake mogul from scratch!

ACKNOWLEDGEMENTS

A very special thank you to those who have supported my journey and helped me turn my dreams into a reality...

Dr. Sheva Quinn; Alphonso Quinn; Bertha (Cookie) Rush; Linda Belk; William (Rickey) Perkins; Maurice and Minnie Thompson; Tiffany Heard; Dixie Ann Jones; Melanie Holley; Sherrnill Jones-Foster; Lisa Favors; Kim Snipes; Krystal White; Kwanza Lincoln; Derrick Russell; Marla Roberts; Lavina Fawn McQueen; Vincent Crawford; Janice Presha; Chrystal Harvey

Chapter X. Your Dreams Matter Start Where You Are with What You Have

Olivia St.Vil

www.livybelle.com
Facebook.com/livybellsews
Instagram.com/livybellesews
Twitter.com/livybellesews

Olivia Grace St.Vil is an 8-year-old entrepreneur who discovered her love of fashion at an early age. A Haitian-Ugandan American raised in the suburbs of Maryland, she decided she wanted to become a fashion designer at the age of 5. Her parents bought her first sewing machine at age 6, and Olivia had her first sewing lesson with her grandmother shortly thereafter.

Livy Belle was created in 2018 so that Olivia could begin sharing her love of sewing and fashion with the world. Her first product was inspired by a trip to Walt Disney World with her family. After she and her mom could not find interchangeable bows they loved for a set of Minnie Mouse ears they received, she decided to make her own. She wanted to make something she could wear every day, whether at Disney or not.

Olivia is looking forward to launching more new products within the Livy Belle brand but is very excited with her first product launch of her custom hair accessories. Her favorite parts are being able to pick out the fabrics and creating the final product.

Between her homeschool co-op classes and lessons with her next-door neighbor, she has been spending time perfecting her craft. In her first 6 months, she learned to make a pocketbook, pillow, apron, skirt, a pair of pants, a bow and more. With her scrap material, she enjoys making clothes for her baby dolls as well.

Olivia has a big brother, 11, a little sister, 7, and two loving parents. With the help of her mom, who is also an entrepreneur, she launched her Instagram page before launching her first product. While mommy helps to co-manage, she produces the content and responds to all of the comments (unless otherwise noted).

The inspiration behind starting her own business comes from her desire to give back to the homeless in the form of clothes. Her ultimate dream is to open up her own fashion design boutique and travel the world making clothes for the homeless.

In her spare time, she enjoys playing with her dolls, taking Taekwondo (in which she just received her black belt) and spending time with her family and friends.

What is your favorite quote that can be printed on a T-shirt, written on a mirror or wall?

My favorite quote is, "Mistakes are proof that you are trying." (Unknown)

What are the 6 major ingredients or components that have contributed to the formulation of your success as a young change-maker thus far?

My first ingredient is my mom because she showed me a video on YouTube on how to sew bows, and she believed that I could do it. So, I did! Next is my grandma because she was the first person who taught me how to sew. And when she comes to visit, she helps me to get better at sewing and learn proper ways to use my machine. My Auntie Julian is another person who has contributed to my success, because she is always checking on my work, and she helps to show me how to make my bows better.

I also love to post on Instagram because that's how I've been able to get customers and meet other kidpreneurs like me. YouTube is a key ingredient because that's how I get inspiration to make new things, including clothes for my dolls. It also teaches me how to fix my sewing machine if it gets jammed.

My neighbor, Ms. Jennifer, has been a huge supporter and contributes to my success because she taught me how to read patterns and helped me to make my first pocketbook, skirt and pair of pants. She gave me a new sewing machine and a lot of other supplies to help me run my business.

My mom's friend, Tara Darnley of Dreams Inspire Reality, threw me an online "Biz Shower" and her Facebook group purchased and sent so many items from my Amazon wishlist that I needed for my business, to help me make my dreams come true. They sent everything from a sewing table, a sewing chair to sit on, lots of thread, storage containers, sewing scissors and more! I'm so thankful.

I will always remember having this many people to support and believe in my business.

What does your typical business or work day look like? When do you fit in fun, school, friends and family?

Because I'm homeschooled, it makes it easier for me to fit in fun, school, friends and family. I'm able to have a more flexible schedule on a typical day. I usually start working on my school work and chores after breakfast. Once that's finished, I start working on my Livy Belle business.

I take martial arts and just received my black belt with my sister, brother and mom. I also like to hang out with my friends and cousins. And I get to spend time doing that, too. Being a new kidpreneur, I'm learning that sometimes, I have to skip playing in order to get my work done. But my business is also fun for me.

What would you say success means to you? Why is it so important?

Success means to me to accomplish something and finish what you started. It's important to me because I want to become a fashion designer and make clothes for the homeless. And to accomplish my goal, I have to make sure I don't give up on my success.

How important would you say it is to be connected to other young people doing amazing things? How did you make these connections?

When I see other kids doing amazing things, it inspires me to do amazing things too. It keeps me inspired and reminds me that I can do anything. Not too long ago, I was able to inspire my friend and help her come up with ideas to start her business, too.

I make these connections mostly because my mom makes a lot of friends through her blog and social media, and their kids become my friends too. My mom also showed me how to connect with other young people on social media using Instagram. It's fun seeing other kidpreneurs!

How important would you say reading and research is to the success of your business? What 3 business books would you recommend?

I would say reading and research is 100 percent important because it helps me to understand what customers want. And it helps me to provide a better product and service.

The three business books I would recommend are ***Whose Shoes Are You Wearing?*** by my mom and my Auntie Julian because it teaches you to, "Do it afraid." Sometimes you have to do things that scare you.

Number two, ***The CEO book: Cleo Edison Oliver, The Playground Millionaire*** by Sundee T. Frazier, because it teaches you to never give up even when you have a lot of challenges in your business.

The number three book would be The American Girl book ***Be Forever Melody – No Ordinary Sound***, because the lesson is to find your own voice in everything you do because we are all unique.

If you could advise a future young mogul to do 3 things before starting their business what would they be?

The three lessons I would share with other young moguls to do before starting their own business would be:

Number one: Find a business that you really want to do and have fun doing it.

Number two: Start marketing your business and building a buzz before your product is ready. My mom had me make bows for her when she was going to Disney. So people kept asking her where she got them from, and that's how I got my first orders (before I even had a website or Instagram account),

Lastly, don't wait until everything is perfect or in order. My mom helped me start my Instagram account before I had created my bows or a way for people to purchase them. She was able to start getting email addresses so when I was ready to start selling, I had people already interested in buying. It showed me there was a market for what I wanted to sell.

What are 3 lessons you have learned so far as a CEO, Founder or Public Figure?

The three lessons I have learned are:

1. A lot of times you'll have to work on your business even when you may want to do other things

2. You still have to take your business seriously even though you can have fun with it.

3. Always do the best that you can do, even when no one is watching

Where do you pull inspiration from? Person, place or thing

I pull my inspiration from my grandmother and my neighbor Ms. Jennifer because they sew just like me. I also really love Disney, so I pull inspiration through some of the fabrics I choose. YouTube also inspires me because I'm learning how to make clothes for my dolls and other fun things. I'm also inspired because my Mom is an entrepreneur, so I watch her work even when she's tired. I also watch and have done interviews with her on live stream, so it is helping me feel more comfortable with video.

What are 3 specific challenges you have had as a young mogul? How have you been able to overcome them?

One challenge I had was not making all of the bows the same. I overcame that challenge by making my own pattern, so they are all the same size. Another challenge I had was wasting fabric and thread because the strings would get stuck in my machine. I overcame that challenge by creating samples of the product first and testing out new fabrics and new threads. The last challenge is working when I want to play with my friends and siblings. I overcome that challenge by thinking about my business and my customers. I want to make them happy, so they will continue to support me.

What are your goals for the future? What's next?

My goals are to add more products to the Livy Belle line by making pocketbooks, skirts and pants. My biggest long-term goal is to open up a fashion design store and to find a way to provide clothes for homeless people around the world.

I am a mini fashionista who loves to sew, and I started my business at 8 years old. My mission is to help other young girls fall in love with their own unique sense of style. In my business, I help girls who love fashion and Disney find the perfect accessory for their next outing or Disney adventure. I am also a homeschooled a black belt in Taekwondo, and I love arts and crafts and hanging out with my family. I hope to be able to work with you and help you find your next fashion accessory for yourself or for someone you love.

ACKNOWLEDGEMENTS

A very special thank you to those who have supported my journey

and helped me turn my dreams into a reality...

Phillip & Christine St.Vil; Fidelia Namirembe; Don and Tanya Barnett; Heather Parsons; Michael St.Vil; Mary Kiganda; Eric Kareem; Kimberly McKissick; Pastors Charles & Cynthia Williams; Keianna Johnson Laila & Maya Cole; Nevaeh & Christian Skeeter; Cal and Renee Coakley; Shantae, Kennedy & Mikayla; Pelt; Shanise N. Griffith; Sherrill Mosee; Tara Darnley; Nourah Shuaibi; Marlene St.Vil; George & Agnes Kiganda

Chapter XI. Young and Motivated with Pretty Nails
Bailee Knighten

www.BaileesNailBox.com
Facebook.com/BaileesNailBox
Instagram.com/BaileesNailBox

When Bailee was 6 years old, she asked her mom for a nail stand. Similar to a lemonade stand, she set it up in front of her house and provided manicures for $5. She enjoyed it so much; people started making appointments for Bailee to come over to do their little girls' nails.

Bailee Knighten was born and raised in Atlanta, Ga. In 2016, her family moved to Tampa, Fl. Being new to the area, she didn't have many friends yet but still wanted to make little girls smile with her nail designs. Together with her mother, they came up with Bailee's Nail Box. It was a great way for her to create fun designs for little girls everywhere.

Bailee's Nail Box was officially started on Jan. 3, 2017, with a mission to always make little girls smile with new and creative nail designs that create lasting memories. Bailee was 9 years old. She wanted to create and sell nail boxes so little girls could enjoy the perks of making fun designs in the comfort of their own home.

Since starting Bailee's Nail Box, she has had amazing opportunities to speak at the Brown Girl Magic Conference, Me & Mommy Dream Bigger Tour, and the Inspiring Greatness Conference.

In October 2017, Bailee's Nail Box was one of three finalists in the Wells Fargo Pitch Perfect Contest to pitch for $5,000 in Miami.

Outside of running a business, Bailee has a passion for track and field. She and her teammates set a record in the state of Georgia for the 4x100 8-9-year-old age group. Her passion for school is a top priority, as good grades always come first. In addition to consistently being on the honor roll, she represented her school in the 4th grade science competition at the Museum of Science and Industry.

Being that she is the only girl and middle child, Bailee is competitive in nature, she is always up for a good game or contest. Bailee also enjoys horseback riding, gymnastics, and swimming.

What is your favorite quote that can be printed on a T-shirt, written on a mirror or wall?

My favorite quote is "Always try your best, no matter what."

What are the 6 major ingredients or components that have contributed to the formulation of your success as a young change-maker thus far?

1. **Hard work** - When you have a business, there is always something you can do to get better. I'm learning that the work doesn't stop.

2. **Not giving up** - It's easy to give up when things get hard. However, if you love what you do, you will not want to quit. I'm glad I have the support of my family that motivates me to continue to work my business.

3. **Research** - This allows me to know what's working, or not working, in my business. Research tells me what the customers want and what products to order. I'm learning that research is necessary to be successful in my business, because the information you learn can save you time and money.

4. **Not doing it alone** - My mom helps me with my business. My dad and brothers support me as I work my business. They come to my events and share my business with their friends. Although my name is on the box, it feels like a real family affair. I couldn't do anything without the help of my family, and I'm very grateful.

5. **Share your story** - People love knowing what, when, how and why you started your business. What's the story behind why you created your business? What did you have to go through to get to where you are? I've learned that when you share your story, people connect with you on a different level. I love telling young girls how I started

80

Bailee's Nail Stand at 6 years old, then starting Bailee's Nail Box at 9. There were a few changes that had to happen to transition to where I am today, but that's part of the story I share as well. I want girls to know that you can do what you put your mind to. If you have the support of your parents (or guardians), that's even better.

6. **Know your numbers** - When you have a business, it's all about the numbers. It's almost like you have to become an expert in math, or at least that is what it feels like. I need to know what gross, net, profit, loss, inventory cost, sales, discounts, percentages mean, and more. It's nice to have a cool product and sell it to people, but you have to know how much you're making if you want to stay in business.

What does your typical business or work day look like? When do you fit in fun, school, friends and family?

After school, I come home and ask my mother if we have any new sales. If we do, I help box them and go to the post office and ship them out. If we don't have new sales, we talk about the business and think of new designs. During the week, I'm not allowed to watch TV, so I finish my homework first and then go track practice. My parents do a great job of supporting my business, school events, and social activities.

What would you say success means to you? Why is it so important?

Success to me means having a rewarding business and having all the things I need. I desire to be a good person, always try my best and have tons of fun. Of course, I want my business to be great, but I want to enjoy the journey to greatness as well.

It's important to be successful because you get many opportunities that can change your life and make your business greater than it is.

How important would you say it is to be connected to other young people doing amazing things? How did you make these connections?

It's important to have friends that are also kidpreneurs because it allows me to learn how they run their business, give each other advice and bounce news ideas off of. I've met some very cool kidpreneurs by attending many kid-focused conferences. I've been fortunate enough to speak at the same conference that Gabrielle Goodwin of Gabby Bows was the keynote. I've also met, Moziah "Mo" Bridges, creator of Mo's Bows, and Mikaila Ulmer, creator of Bee Sweet Lemonade.

Meeting these young moguls motivate me to keep trying when I'm down or doubting myself. I keep moving forward.

How important would you say reading and research is to the success of your business? What 3 business books would you recommend?

It's important to always read because as a kidpreneur, we don't know everything, and we are still learning in every area of our lives. My mom always says, "Leaders are readers." Reading allows me to learn from other successful business owners and hopefully avoid some mistakes. Research helps your business, because it allows you to learn what you don't know and what your customer wants from you.

1. *Better Than a Lemonade Stand! Small Business Ideas for Kids* by Daryl Bernstein

2. *Entrepreneurship: Create Your Own Business with 25 Projects* by Alex Kahan

3. *Rich Dad's Escape from the Rat Race: How to Become a Rich Kid by Following Rich Dad's Advice Book* by Robert Kiyosaki

If you could advise a future young mogul to do 3 things before starting their business what would they be?

1. What is your business name? Pick a name that you will be happy with 15-20 years from now. What is the meaning behind it? Is it clear what your business is, or will you always have to explain it?
2. Why do you want to start a business? Do you think you could do this for 5 years or more? Do you want to start a business to change people's lives, minds, or both? How will your business stand out or be different?
4. Is your business a product or service? Will your business be a one-time buy or something that people will come back again and again for?

What are 3 lessons have learned so far as a CEO, founder or public figure?

1. You have to be consistent with your business.
2. Excellent customer service should be your top priority.

3. You can always be a better business owner.

Where do you pull inspiration from?

I get inspiration from my mom. She inspires me because she helps me keep my business going. My mom also has her own business, and I wanted to start my business because I saw my mom running her own.

What are 3 specific challenges you have had as a young mogul? How have you been able to overcome them?

1. **Coming up with new designs** - When we first started, we had a few designs. Sometimes it's challenging to come up with more designs. That's when I go into research mode and look all around me for inspiration.
2. **Marketing** - I first had to learn what marketing was. My mom told me, it's selling. My boxes are created for girls ages 4 -12, however, their moms are the ones buying the box. So, I needed to learn how to sell to mothers and not little girls.
4. **Learning how to run an online business** - When I started my business, it was a nail stand in front of my house. When I started selling my boxes online, I found out it was a lot more work. I'm grateful my mother had the patience to help me and teach me certain things step by step about the back-end and technical part of my site.

What are your goals for the future? What's next?

I want to finish school and become a nurse. As far as Bailee's Nail Box, I would love to open my own nail store and/or salon and create at least 100 different designs. Currently, we are working on new boxes and strongly considering the idea of becoming a subscription box service.

I am a business owner and I started my business at 9 years old. My mission is to always make little girls smile with new and creative nail designs that create lasting memories. In my business, I help girls explore their creative side while spending valuable time with the most important people in their lives. I also am a lifelong learner, people person, dependable and forever a daddy's girl. I hope to be able to work with you and help you and your child learn about creating a business that makes a difference.

ACKNOWLEDGEMENTS

A very special thank you to those who have supported my journey and helped me turn my dreams into a reality...

Earl & Bernetta Knighten; Corrine Lenoir; Delores Knighten; Martha Mitchell; Szana Marr; Earline King; Carlotta Ellis; Anthony & Angela Early; Edwin & Teresa Williams; Aseelah Knighten; Vivian Knighten; Brandi Riley; LaTasha Daniels; Jenae Calloway; Choya Porter Melody Sturgis; Brenda Palmer

Chapter XII. A Chef's Recipe for Success
Chef Simone Bridges

www.goddessfoodfactory.com
Facebook.com/goddessfoodjax
Instagram.com/goddessfoodjax
Twitter.com/goddessfoodjaxc
Linkedin.com/in/simonebridges

Simone Bridges, born in Jacksonville, Fla., is a popular kid chef and the owner of Goddess Food Factory. She is well known for her unique twist on traditional desserts, cooking classes and fun-filled birthday parties at her shop. Her delicious pastries have received rave reviews by celebrities, chefs and residents in Jacksonville and beyond. On October 30, 2017, Chef Simone was featured on Steve Harvey's talk show, "Steve", where she shared her recipe for success and she showed him how to make her famous Snickers Brownies.

As a student at Darnell-Cookman School of the Medical Arts, her love for science and mathematics has also earned her the nickname of the "STEM Chef." Due to an overwhelming number of requests for her recipes and her love for STEM, she created the ExS.T.R.E.A.M. Baking Program, and shortly after the ExS.T.R.E.A.M. Baking Subscription Boxes came into existence. They are monthly subscription boxes in which she infuses baking and cooking with Science, Technology, Reading, Engineering, Arts and Mathematics.

As a motivational speaker, Simone has spoken to audiences of all ages about STEM/STREAM, her appreciation for food, and entrepreneurship. She was the keynote speaker for Girlz Rock of Ft. Wayne, Indiana and has served on several panels. In the summer of 2017, Chef Simone expanded her skills into writing about her love for unique foods. She became a junior chef columnist for Afrik Kalabash Magazine, devoted to celebrating the uniqueness of African taste. Chef Simone is currently working on her very first cookbook.

Although she's only 12 years old, she has already begun to build a strong culinary resume. Simone is the youngest winner in the seven-year history of the Taste of Black Competition. She has been featured on the cover of Inspiring magazine and River City Live, and she has participated in major food festivals. Additionally, Chef Simone was also one of ten kids featured in LeBron James' "Always Believe" campaign. She's no stranger to television, either. She appears in three Smile of a Child commercials that are broadcasted globally on Trinity Baptist Network. Way to Go, Chef! This pastry princess has stated that her vision is to inspire other young kids around the world to never give up, and to Think STREAM Big. Ultimately, her goal is to continue sharing her love of baking, and to one day establish a nonprofit organization with the main focus of empowering and growing kid entrepreneurs.

What is your favorite quote that can be printed on a T-shirt, written on a mirror or wall?

I often say, "Dream Big and Never Give Up." It's one of my favorite quotes that I use on a regular basis to motivate myself to dream bigger than big. When I face difficult challenges, or when I'm having a hard time like trying to create a new dessert, I remind myself to work harder so that I can accomplish my initial goal. Sometimes I struggle, and I know that everything doesn't always come out perfect on the first try, or even the second or third, but I never give up. I just think of a different way to reach my goal. Sometimes I get someone to assist me, or take a brain break and come back to it at a later time. I also found that just simply breaking the task down into smaller steps that I can definitely achieve helps a lot. The phrase, "Dream Big and Never Give Up" is posted on a canvas in my room and serves as a daily reminder to reach for higher goals, and that once I start something, to see it through to the end.

What are the 6 major ingredients or components that have contributed to the formulation of your success as a young change-maker thus far?

If I had to choose six major components that contributed to the formulation of my success, I would say one, my faith, because I have a strong faith and I pray over my business, over my family, over my successes and over all of my challenges. I ask God to show me how to do it right. How I can do better? I also have faith that I'm making right decisions. As a young entrepreneur, I don't know everything. I seek advice from my parents and other people who I have faith in. However, most of the time, I make the final decision. So, I pray about it and go for it.

Secondly, identifying and knowing my passion has been a major part of my success. What is my gift in this world? I know I love science, singing and dancing, but most importantly, baking has always been a passion of mine. I've been baking since I was 3 years old. I bake all the time. It's my gift, and I literally want to share it with everyone. That's why I have baking classes at my shop. I teach kids the fundamentals and science behind baking. We also have lot of fun, and kids enjoy making and eating treats. Baking is such a big part of my life. One of my favorite things to do is to hang with other chefs, because we can literally talk about food all day.

The third thing is motivation. I motivate myself every morning. It might sound crazy, but I wake up and I give myself a pep talk. When I'm struggling, I create a growth mindset and positive energy so that I can accomplish any goal. Plus, I'm lucky enough to have family and friends who motivate me to do my best. Self-motivation helps me prepare for speaking engagements, or to facilitate culinary classes. I go on stage and nail it.

The fourth contribution would be marketing. My mama has always told me to think of myself as a walking billboard for my brand. Since I'm not on any billboard (yet), I wear my brand everywhere that I go. I wear Goddess Food Factory flip-flops when go to the nail salon to get a pedicure. When I go to major functions, I wear my signature pink chef attire, and the guests will say, "Oh, that's Chef Simone Bridges." "Oh, yeah. She's the baker." I'm always getting approached in the grocery store or the movies because people recognize me when I'm always wearing my Goddess Food Factory T-shirts. Many times, the logo will inspire conversation with people and provide opportunities for me to talk about my business. Either way, I'm always branding myself with my Goddess Food Factory custom clothes, backpacks and other fashions.

Networking would be the fifth contribution. Networking can be a little scary sometimes. Many times, I'm the only kid at seminars, but I never let that stop me. One strategy that I learned was to introduce myself to people, have my pitch ready and give out my business card. So, everywhere that I go, I always walk up to them and say, "Hi. I'm Chef Simone Bridges, and I'm the owner of Goddess Food Factory and ExSTREAM Baking." I pitch my business and ask them the name of their business, what are they doing, and why they love doing it. I've learned to really listen and make connections with them. I love networking, giving and receiving advice and discussing how we can help each other's business. That's why networking is just so important.

Last, but not least, continuous learning is a major contributor to the success of any business. I love attending workshops, and I love learning new things, new techniques and new ways to grow my business. The secret to learning is listening, paying full attention and taking action. Research - there's so much to learn. The Internet has an enormous amount of resources; from YouTube, webinars, Facebook groups and so much more. I also learn a lot from my mentor, Mrs. Casey Kelley, owner of Blended Designs. She teaches me how to level up and invites me to major summits and conferences. So, continuous learning has played a major role in growing my business. Those would be my six major contributions to the formulation of my success.

What does your typical business or work day look like? When do you fit in fun, school, friends and family?
Like any other kid, I have my normal morning routine. Then, I have my self-motivational pep talk, or I listen to motivational videos on YouTube. It helps to create a positive go-getter tone for the day. My workday begins early in the morning. I always post a motivational quote in my Instagram stories to inspire others. It would be something similar to, "Believe in yourself. You can achieve any goal that you want to achieve," or, "Dream Big and Never Give Up." It's a way for me to pass my positive energy on to others. After that, I'm off to school to gain more knowledge and to chill with my friends. I'm really into sports, so depending on the season, I may have track, basketball or cheer practice after school. Sports allow me to have a social life and to connect with my friends. I complete my homework when I'm waiting on my coach or when I arrive home. On days that I don't have practice, I go to my shop, Goddess Food Factory, and I work for a couple of hours. I do everything from checking inventory to making sales. On the weekend is when I go into full work mode. I'm usually booked for cooking classes, birthday parties or

speaking engagements, so I travel a lot. I've learned to take advantage of opportunities to sleep. I used to be on my cell phone or talking to my sister, Jasmine, when I'm traveling, but now I rest my body whenever I can. Another great tip that I learned is to take snacks and bottles of water with me. Being a kidpreneur is fast-paced at times, therefore being prepared eliminates a lot of possible problems. Trust me, I had to learn the hard way on a few occasions.

What would you say success means to you? Why is it so important?
For me, success is a feeling that you get of pure joy. It's something that you feel on the inside, and you know when it happens because it feels so awesome. For example, I was on "Steve" with Steve Harvey. Never in a million years would I have thought that there would be a title that says, "12-year-old baker, Chef Simone Bridges, meets Steve Harvey." My family and I have been watching the Steve Harvey on television for, like, all my life. I would've never thought that I would be on there. When the producers called me to be on his show, I was shocked. My family and I couldn't believe it. We were so happy. We were jumping up and down, and that's what success feels like. The phone call itself was success. Just having the opportunity to go was so joyful.

I remember envisioning what my episode would look like and what I would say to Mr. Harvey when I meet him. I was debating on which chef coat to wear? Long sleeve or short sleeve? So many thoughts raced through my mind. So many emotions came over my body. I had moments of fear and moments that I could tackle the world all at the same time. As the days grew closer for me to fly to Los Angeles, I knew that everything that I had accomplished prior to that moment, had prepared me for ultimate success. I felt it in my heart and I was ready. Nothing could stop me. I was so proud of myself.

When the day came that I met Mr. Harvey, it was another successful moment. He's super funny and he made me feel right at home (on the big stage, LOL). The big part came when I was able to watch myself on a nationally syndicated television show alongside a major celebrity. How could I not feel successful? My excitement level was at a level ten. I felt successful each step of the way though. That was also the moment in which I realized that I had to start dreaming bigger, and that I can achieve any goal that I worked hard for. Once you get a taste of success, it makes you feel like you can change the world. I value all successes because they are all important to my growth. Small accomplishments help me reach major goals. Within a task, my first little step is a success and the last step is a success. Every single step is a success. And that's what success means to me. The feeling is like, "Oh my God, I've really done this. So, when I feel that way, I enjoy the moment, because it's a beautiful feeling.

How important would you say it is to be connected to other young people doing amazing things? How did you make these connections?

Building relationships and making connections is huge. I would say that it is very important to be connected to other young people doing amazing things, because we learn from each other. We understand similar struggles. We can share insights about our business and share resources. Kids love to learn from kids. We know how each other thinks and we can relate to each other. We exchange phone numbers and make new friends; a new business friend and maybe even create a partnership or collaborate on a project. They might even connect me to people that I've never met and vice versa. Creating solid relationships could be the difference in them referring you for a project that they didn't feel fit their brand. Plus, kids in the business celebrate and congratulate each other more. They're doing amazing things, and you're doing amazing things, and it's just great. You learn to encourage each other, too, if someone is having a bad day. It happens. So, it's really good to make connections with other industry kids. I meet other kidpreneurs at kid expos, speaking engagements and sometimes when they contact me in DM through social media. I contact them back and them we continue to communicate. Easy peasy!

How important would you say reading and research is to the success of your business? What 3 business books would you recommend?

Reading and research is very important to the success of my business because everything that I know is either coming from hands-on learning, researching or reading. I'm always researching to see how I can make a dessert better or find substitutes for people who have certain allergies. For example, applesauce makes for a great substitution for eggs. Researching is important because you can find new recipes for simple things, like how to make ice cream. How to make homemade crust. Like, there's so much business knowledge that can come from researching. I research a lot to grow certain areas of my business, and to learn new tips for various things.

As a youth STREAM advocate, I'm always promoting the importance of reading. As an avid reader, I read for pleasure, business, self-care or simply because I feel like it. I read all kinds of books. Some books help me to reinforce my baking skills, to gather information about creating systems & processing structures, or to become a better speaker. I'm always learning better ways to stay healthy and how to improve my business. Reading is like discovering a whole new world at my fingertips. The cool thing about it is that I can revisit anytime that I choose to. Many times, I gain new knowledge from rereading that I missed during the first read.

One business book that I would recommend is ***101 ways to relax and reduce stress*** by Candy Paull. This is such a great book, oh my gosh, because it teaches you how to calm down and relax when conflicts arise. One tip that I would recommend is tip number 27, and it says to keep a gratitude journal. In that gratitude journal, you're supposed to write down things that you are thankful for. It's basically like a self-motivator. So, when you feel like your kind of down and in a sad mood, you can look back in your gratitude journal and read everything that you have accomplished and everything that you are thankful for. It'll cheer you up. In business, it's very important that you know how to de-stress yourself and to relax. Juggling classwork, wanting to hang out with friends, and doing household chores while being a kid entrepreneur is not always easy. Not to mention playing sports or other activities. Yes, the struggle really gets real at times. Although I have a solid support team, having a bank of tools to reduce my own stress has been a mega bonus. Plus, when I'm relaxed I perform better.

Another book that I would recommend is, ***1,001 ways to market your yourself and your small business*** by Lisa Shaw. Tip number 319 says, "If you're advertising a business in a card pack, it may be worth the extra placement fee to get your card inserted in the top of the pack." This is a really great marketing tip, because most people only look at what's on top or in the front of something, and then they stop reading or looking.

Marketing is such an important component to the growth of a business. It can also be costly depending on the method that's chosen. I've learned several ways to market my business using no or low-cost methods from this book. The tips are easy and kid-friendly. They also apply to any business.

As a chef, my third suggestion is not really a book, but it's a subscription to Food Network Magazine because I learn new recipes every single issue. I learn about foods from around the world and get plating ideas, and it helps to keep me up with current food trends. So those are the three business books that I would recommend.

If you could advise a future young mogul to do 3 things before starting their business what would they be?
Based on my experience, the three things that I would recommend to a future young mogul before starting their business is to first, identify your passion or your gift. You definitely want to make sure it's something that you love doing and want to do very often. Make sure it's something that you are willing to share with others, and something that you would know a lot about. You will have to pitch your business to multiple people continuously, so make sure that you're prepared. Learn as many aspects of your business as possible. This is your business, and if you don't know what's going on, then others may not see your business' full value and potential.

Secondly, you want to get a good support team of motivators because you want to make sure you're able to go to them for advice. I love positive energy around me. It keeps me going, and I think better that way. I love when my family and I have power meetings. We generate great ideas and the mood is always right for brainstorming. When things can get really hectic, having people who can help me create solutions makes everything better. Plus, everybody loves praise. It makes me feel good when my work is acknowledged. I feel successful. So, get a great group of people whose opinions you value, and who will uplift you when times get tough.

Lastly, I suggest watching a lot of growth mindset videos, because you always need to think positive. I love listening to Mr. Mario Armstrong, host of the Never Settle Show. He's my personal favorite because he motivates me while teaching me business strategies. He's a two-time Emmy winner and very knowledgeable. What I like most about mindset videos is that they have not only changed my way of thinking toward my business, but I don't let other things bother me as much. I try to learn from my mistakes and focus on the positive portion of the situation. There is a bright side to everything. Think glass-half-full versus half-empty.

What are 3 lessons you have learned so far as a CEO, founder or public figure?

92

There's a saying, "Sometimes you win and sometimes you learn." As the CEO of Goddess Food Factory, I've learned several valuable lessons that have played major roles in the success of my business. As previously stated, the importance of being my own walking billboard is one lesson that I learned. I was in Miami, speaking with Ms. Corporate America, Elizabeth Garcia. She's also the owner of Elizabeth's Secret Beauty Bar. I was telling her about my business. She asked me what products I sold and so forth. So I began to share all of the items: baking subscription boxes, mittens, aprons, hats, backpacks, T-shirts ... and then she stopped me. She questioned, "Why aren't you wearing one of your shirts with your brand on it, instead of promoting someone else's brand? You are advertising for them instead of yourself." At that very moment, I knew she was correct, because my mom tells me the same thing all of the time and I didn't listen. And there I was, at a very important business event with several influencers and if I had chosen to simply brand myself, I would have exposed several people to my logo, even if I didn't have a moment to get a one-on-one conversation with them. Since then, I stay branded, especially at functions of any kind. I keep business cards on me, and I give them to everybody. Everybody knows somebody that knows somebody.

Another lesson that I learned is probably the most important lesson of all: Protect your brand and your image. I do consider myself a child of God, but I am still a kid who is very outgoing, especially around my friends. One day, a friend of mine had a sleepover and we were all dancing and posting videos on Musically. One of the videos that she posted, I was twerking. I had just learned how to do it from my friends, and we were all just 12-year-old girls having innocent fun. Well, that's what I thought at the time. Luckily and unluckily, my parents follow all of my social medias AND most of my friends' social medias, too. The bad part is that unknowingly my dad, Elgin Bridges, saw the video that was posted on one of my friend's accounts. I knew better than to post anything like that. Around 11:00 p.m. that same night, my dad called me and told me to pack my stuff because he was coming to pick me up from the sleepover. At the time I didn't know why. I thought something was wrong at home or with a family member. I wasn't due to go home until the following day, so I kept asking him why he was picking me up. He said that he'd talk to me once he saw me. Once he arrived at my friend's house, I knew that something was terribly wrong because he had a look on his face that was unfamiliar to me. My dad is my best friend, and his eyes always light up when we're together. Once we reached home from the silent car ride, I would soon hear the answer to this mystery. At that time, I still didn't know what was wrong, but I knew it had to be something really bad. It was now almost midnight and my father woke up my mom. We all sat down in the living room. My dad put his arms around me and started praying. I started crying because I thought that something happened to my sister, Jasmine, because she wasn't a part of this mystery, spiritual meeting. After praying, my dad asked me for my cell phone. I didn't know why he needed it, but I took it out of my satchel and handed it to him. He gave it back and told me to pull up so-and-so's Musically account. While standing in front of him and my mom, I pulled it up and saw the video of me twerking with my friends, and another one of just me twerking by myself. You won't believe what happened. I fainted. PLOP, right on the floor. It's funny now, but it wasn't then. Long story short, after ensuring that I was OK, my parents explained to me that I could potentially damage my image by doing things that I shouldn't do at my age. I was so embarrassed, and I immediately apologized. Yes, I was only having fun, but my parents were right. The good part is that my dad saw it before any of my major business partners did. Plus, the next day I told my friend what happened and she deleted the video from her account. We all do things that we shouldn't do. It's life and that's how we learn, but we can also prevent some things from occurring by learning from other people's mistakes. So, learn from my mistake and protect your image. You have to be extra aware of what could potentially harm your business.

The last lesson is more or less some advice versus a lesson. Treat people with respect, make contributions that will make the world a better place and always have good-quality products. I have a lot of repeat customers, they brag about how friendly I am, and they tell me that my Snickers Brownies always taste so good. I put my heart into when I bake, and I want everyone to feel at home. I love to see the reaction when someone bites into any of my treats. Sometimes the reactions are so funny, because the customers dance, groan, and be like, "Woo chile." LOL I just giggle. My ExS.T.R.E.A.M. baking subscription boxes and my educational program have consistently been huge hits, too. I travel around the United States speaking to other kids about the importance of STEM/STREAM careers. The kids are always actively engaged, which makes the teachers and principals happy.

Where do you pull inspiration from?
I'm extremely fortunate that I come from a family of entrepreneurs. Lavish Moments Weddings, Events & Rentals is our family business

which is led by my mom, Arica Bridges. In addition, my grandmother owns Glory Cakes & Pastries. So, I learned how to be a kid boss at an early age from them. I pull a lot of inspiration from my grandma, Phyllis Harris. We're always creating new desserts. I like to experiment and figure out how to create new twists on traditional treats. She teaches me how to make desserts the traditional way, and then I ponder on what to add to it. Sometimes, we bounce ideas off of each other. I love adding peaches and pecans to a lot of different desserts. It often gives a unique taste to the desserts that my customers and I like. Fresh fruit is seasonal, so we like to change it up and use only the best ingredients. My grandma has a lot of patience, but she doesn't like to waste food. So, I can't experiment too much when I'm with her. However, when I get home, I'll try over and over again until I feel like I have the perfect blend of ingredients. I'm kind of like a palate princess. My taste buds are very fine, and I have a niche for combining unusual ingredients together to create delicious masterpieces.

I also get a lot of inspiration when I'm at my bakery, Goddess Food Factory. I think about all future new products that I'm going to make, and what my bakery will look like in the future. It would be a building that screams "fun" from the road. Girls are going to want to come inside to see what's going on. The outside and inside will have picturesque places to take photos. Upon their entrance they'll smell the sweet aromas coming from all of the amazing treats. I will also have a few interactive treats that they can make and design themselves that will not require baking. If they would like to bake, I'll still offer cooking classes in our state-of-the-art kiddie kitchen. I imagine having a separate glam space for manis and pedis. A dress-up and career room would also be a great addition. I envision mirrors with cool affirmations on them in glitter, and a runway that lights up when someone walks on it. And so much more. Goddess Food Factory is already the place to be, but it will soon be a must-see location even for tourists.

There's a quote, "Don't quit your daydream." So many inspiring ideas come from my dreams. I dream of new treats to make and who I would serve them to. In my dreams, I've served Michelle Obama and Ellen Degeneres. After tasting my Snickers Brownies, Ellen started dancing, and I laughed and danced with her. In another dream, I gave cooking classes to Blue Ivy and North West. We had so much fun. I also gave them some of my chef dolls to keep as treasures. Moreover, my dreams allow me to travel the world and speak to other children about accomplishing their dreams. The crowds are huge, and the kids are chanting, "Kids can do anything." One of my speeches that I give now in real life was inspired by a dream. I want to make a great impact on our future, and many times, I get so many great ideas from my dreams. My goal is to inspire and empower kids all over the world.

What are 3 specific challenges you have had as a young mogul? How have you been able to overcome them?
"Challenges are what make life interesting, and overcoming them is what makes life meaningful," said Joshua J. Marine. I like to think of challenges as things that are going to help make my life and the lives of others more meaningful than it was before.

One challenge that I faced as a young mogul was being able to speak in front of large crowds. I used to be very nervous. I would get the sniffles, my palms would get sweaty and my stomach would be in knots. It took prayer and words of encouragement just to get me on the stage. I overcame it with tons of preparation and practice. I watched several videos of other speakers. I learned how to develop three to four speaking points with one overall message. Learning how to get my point across through sharing stories that happened to me allowed for me to be honest and connect with the audience. I became a storyteller on stage. Additionally, I learned to create an acronym to remember my talking points. I still get a little nervous before my speaking engagements, but that's natural. Being prepared empowers me to go and deliver motivational speeches.

Having big dreams can also cause you to want things when the timing is not right. I always come up with new ideas for products and ways to brand my business. Like many other small businesses, a challenge that I face is funding. Although I've learned a lot over time, I'm still learning about the financial portion of my business. When I have an idea, my mom tells me that if I can get the money to fund it, we can try it out, and if it's successful, she'll balance the budget to have money for future purchases. So, I started asking for donations. I wrote down 100 names of people who I could ask to donate $100. It didn't work as plan, but it was a good thought. Most gave donations of various amounts and I was able to raise more than $3,000 to fund my first book, graphics and other promotional marketing ads. I never give up on my dreams and I've learned to be patient and to never give up. I try to focus on one thing at a time. Mr. Mario says, "Start small, learn quick, and scale big." I'm trying to not want everything so fast. Patience may be a virtue, but it's extremely hard as a kid.

Another challenge initially was being a young baker and people not taking me seriously. There were classes that I wanted to take in order to increase my skills, but I wasn't old enough to register for them. Thank Heaven for YouTube, but I really love hands-on trainings. One of the bakers who makes our wedding cakes, Mrs. Earlena, gives me private lessons. She is so much fun to work with, and she's extremely patient with me. She calls me Little Einstein because I learn really fast. A lot of my customers don't believe that I make the treats until they come into the bakery and see me piping frosting on cakes and cupcakes. They are amazed. I'm always amazed that they are still amazed, because I've been doing it for so long. Once they taste the treats, they're completely sold. Mostly, everyone around town knows that I bake now, so I no longer have anything to prove. I just like to wow them with the taste of my treats.

What are your goals for the future? What's next?
My overall goal is to empower other kids to follow their dreams and to believe that they can do anything. With Goddess Food Factory, I definitely see my dream bakery happening with additional products, bedding, clothing, and so much more. The possibilities are endless, and I'm totally ready for everything that comes my way. In addition, I envision myself on the big screen, featured on more nationally syndicated shows, hosting my own cooking show and traveling the world speaking to kids. I will continue being an advocate for STEM/STREAM activities and careers. I want to write several dessert books, cookbooks and story books. I also desire to teach other kids how to write their own books to tell their stories. Moreover, I aspire to start a foundation for girls. I picture teaching them how to become kid entrepreneurs and the importance of helping others. I will host classes to build their self-esteem, and to teach them the power of collaboration. I firmly believe that we are stronger together. I aim to be a moral citizen and to help make the world a better place. I just plan to keep Leveling Up and help create more youth leaders.

I am Chef Simone Bridges, owner of Goddess Food Factory and I started my business at 11 years old. My vision is to inspire and motivate the youth to Never Give Up, and to "Think STREAM Big." In my business, I help youth ages 6-14 learn how to bake using STREAM concepts and find their passion. I also am a singer, dancer, athlete and gifted student. I hope to be able to work with you and help you discover the entrepreneur and leader within.

ACKNOWLEDGEMENTS

A very special thank you to those who have supported my journey

and helped me turn my dreams into a reality...

Elgin & Arica Bridges; Jasmine Bridges; Grannie Phyllis Williams Harris; Dinitra Williams; Ronda Williams; Maliaha Dixon; Derrick Meadows; Chef Sherkenna Buggs; Darrell Stewart; Minister Opal Stewart; Christy Blair; LaTosha Terry; Elizabeth Garcia; Coach Mechelle Canady; Ingenious Basket Creations; Yvonne Singleton Davis; Milagros Cintron; Deja Vu Speaks; Nickholas Butler; Casey Kelley

Chapter XIII. Sweet Success
Christianna Alexander

www.sweetchristis.com
Facebook.com/SweetChristis
Instagram.com/SweetChristis
Twitter.com/sweetchristis
Linkedin.com/in/christianna-alexander

Christianna Alexander was born in Jacksonville, Fla., on Oct. 3, 2005. She is the oldest of three and the daughter of Christopher and Hilda Alexander. Christianna was somewhat of a military brat as a child, as both her parents are Navy veterans. When Christianna started elementary school, her parents began to see her struggle to keep up with her work.

Christianna's learning struggles continued into the second grade. She was ultimately held back, which left her devastated. Christianna refused to give up, and her parents fought hard to get her the help she deserved and needed. Christianna was able to enroll into a school that focused on helping children with learning disabilities like her own. Christianna quickly began to adapt, her confidence began to grow almost overnight and she made the honor roll for the first time ever!

Christianna took her newfound confidence and honed in on her skills of creating and her love for making tasty treats. With her newfound passion, Christianna began baking all sorts of sweets, but found that the baking process came with challenges.

One was the amount of sugar found in many of these treats. Christianna knew she needed to make a change and wanted to provide healthier products but still have fun creating them. With much brainstorming, and lots of trial and error, Christianna created "Sweet Christi's", a company focused on making all-natural handmade soaps that resemble delectable treats like donuts and cupcakes.

Christianna views her disability as a blessing, and her mission in life is to be an ambassador for children everywhere who suffer from learning disabilities. In addition to running her company, she also raises money for a nonprofit to help disadvantaged children learn how to swim. She is an avid swimmer and would like to see childhood downing's eradicated.

What is your favorite quote that can be printed on a T-shirt, written on a mirror or wall?

My favorite quote is, "Stay sweet and never miss a beat." Stay sweet means to always be kind. Never miss a beat means don't give up and always stay strong. I've had my fair share of what I thought to be failures, but I refuse to get bitter or give up. When things are hard, take a deep breath and count down from 5 while telling yourself "I can do this!" Pushing through can be exhausting but in the end, it feels good because you know that you put in the work necessary to accomplish something tough.

What are the 6 major ingredients or components that have contributed to the formulation of your success as a young change-maker thus far?

My six major ingredients that have contributed to my success are: research first, always network, take pictures of everything you do, show the world what you have to offer by tooting your own horn, set up social media accounts (they are free) and to give business cards to EVERYONE.

It is important to research first, so you have information on how to start your business. You will want to know the process, to understand the tools and supplies you may need and to figure out if you even want to do it as a business and move forward.

Networking is important because you can find mentors, friends and even grow your business by using their resources and information they have already learned. You will need pictures to show off your product and behind the scenes. You can then use these pictures on your website, blog or social media. This is a great way to connect with customers. People want to see kids doing great things. This is why it is important to show them exactly that you are doing. Don't be afraid to stand out. Social media is a great way to market your business for FREE. I don't want anyone to run their business without some type of social media account. People will look you up to see what you are up to and this keeps your profit in your pocket. My final tip toe of giving business cards to everyone is VERY important because it helps your customers stay in contact, so they can buy your products and keep up with what you are doing that will help them.

What does your typical business or work day look like? When do you fit in fun, school, friends and family?

I don't have a typical business day. I swim and play the piano throughout the year, so my schedule is really tight. I also will start golf in the fall because I love trying new things. I try to fit all my business stuff in the beginning of my free time, so I can hang out with my friends and family if it's possible. If I can't, it's OK. They understand I'm building something big right now, and it won't be this busy always. When it is time to work I come downstairs, gather all of my supplies and do focused work for a certain amount of time. It varies from day to day depending on what I need to get done and how busy my schedule is. Sometimes I work on making my soaps but there are many other things that I have to do besides making the soaps. I spread my time between making the soap, packaging, organizing my supplies and entering my contacts into the database for my newsletter.

What would you say success means to you? Why is it so important?

Success means having the freedom to purchase whatever you want and to get whatever you need to help others. Can you imagine all of the good I can do in the world with the money I make? It is important to give back, and having a business gives me the opportunity to do just that. None of it matters if I don't use what I have to help others. That is why being successful is so important to me.

How important would you say it is to be connected to other young people doing amazing things? How did you make these connections?

It's very important to stay connected with other young people because you can share your customers and data, and you also collaborate with each other on special projects. The more I talk and tell my story the more I make connections. Everyone has a story to tell and you never know who it will help. These connections make it easier to deal with everyday life as a kid. I make connections at business fairs, expos and anywhere I meet someone doing great things.

How important would you say reading and research is to the success of your business? What 3 business books would you recommend?

Research and reading are very important, but I do not have any general business books that I recommend just yet. One book that I read recently is called *The Lightning Thief*. The main character's name is Percy and in the book he lost his mom but he didn't give up looking. That's what I took out of the book, not to give up, because Percy did not give up on finding his mom. You really can pull insight from books that aren't necessarily about business. The key is to just keep reading everything you can get your hands on. I have a soap book that my mom bought me as a gift when I first started. I use it as a guide to help me label my soaps and make sure I'm legit. I will begin to build my personal library this year with books that will help me to develop into a better person in and out of my business.

If you could advise a future young mogul to do 3 things before starting their business what would they be?

I recommend first, to research and then plan things out. It is easy to think of an idea and start moving but you really have to think things out. Some of my ideas were great and others were not so great. I saved a lot of time and money by researching things first. After doing that, talk it out with your parents. No matter how great the idea is, better to have someone else review it. Your parents are the best place to start being that they are really good resources to use as an investor at startup.

What are 3 lessons have learned so far as a CEO, founder or public figure?

The three lessons I've learned so far is to not give up, always have a clean space and to try to sell most of your products so that you make a profit. In the beginning there is a lot of work and it's not always fun but you have to push through. Having a clean space is key to being organized and productive. It also shows your parents that you are serious and capable of running your own business.

Where do you pull inspiration from?

I pull inspiration from my parents. I see how they talk things out with other people and try to connect with them. They are leaders, especially to me. That makes me feel like I can talk to my customers, or strangers who are interested in me and my business. I also find inspiration in other stores when I'm out shopping. I look for really cool sweets that I can turn into one of my soap creations.

What are 3 specific challenges you have had as a young mogul? How have you been able to overcome them?

The three challenges I had as a young mogul are having dyslexia, being retained in the second grade and having ADHD. I overcame this by first finding new school, GRASP Academy. There, I learn the exact same things as other schools but with different strategies, so I retain it better. It gave a big boost to my self-esteem as well! The school was the best thing for me and I love it. It was very embarrassing to tell people my age and my grade level at first but I'm learning to enjoy the journey I'm on. It is not like everyone else and that is ok. Oh, and also, I use my essential oils to help me daily. I carry them in my bookbag and some of my teachers diffuse them. My family went from living normal American lives to teaching others how to do things naturally. This is one of the reasons my soaps are as natural as possible. I still have a hard time sometimes, but I feel good knowing I have tools to help me improve every day.

What are your goals for the future? What's next?

My goal for the future is to have a studio. I need a functional space, so that I can make my products and get out of my parents' house. I want my space to be inviting, open, and most importantly Fun! When my customers walk in, or when I do an event, I want everyone to leave with a smile on their face. Never in my wildest dreams did I think I would dream of teaching science to others. I've always loved science and to be able to use it to get creative is very exciting which is why I want to share it with other young girls. I also would like to get a mobile food truck with my business logo on it, to transport my products to the many events and expos I plan on attending. I also plan on driving it around to sell my soaps out of at the food truck events. I thought it would be a pretty cool thing to have since my soaps look like sweet treats. My most important goal for the future is to get my soaps into a national retail store. I want to see my soaps in Claire's, Justice, The Gap or some other cool kids boutique. I look forward to mentoring other children on how to be successful as a business owner and be a true mogul. This will happen as I develop more as a speaker. I was also thinking that I could raise more money for charities. I have a very soft spot for the less fortunate, and I always volunteer and lend a helping hand.

I am a kidpreneur and my official title in my company is "Sweet Boss". I started my business at 12 years old. My mission is to inspire children all over the world to follow their dreams and to never give up on their goals. I create natural soap products that look like delectable sweet treats. My products are for everyone young and old and make bath time fun! I am an aquaholic who loves the water and I compete on a local swim team in my hometown. I am also a pianist who plays in multiple recitals every year. I would be honored to work with you and help you achieve all of your dreams and goals.

ACKNOWLEDGEMENTS

A very special thank you to those who have supported my journey and helped me turn my dreams into a reality...

Christopher D. Alexander Sr.; Hilda Alexander; London Alexander; Christopher D. Alexander Jr; Brett Coleman; Hilda Hall; Catherine Franklin; Gwendolyn Holmes; Aaron Holmes; Keshia Alexander; Sean & Tiffany Franklin; Adria Holmes; Kelvin & Cassandra Allen; Monica Triplett; Mr and Mrs Arnett Greene; Joyce Deliphus; James Baptiste; The Smith Family; The Anderson Family; Mr and Mrs Rod Brown

Chapter XIV. You Are the Crown
Lauren A. Harris

www.sparklelee.com

Lauren is an official pageant princess, sweetheart and queen. She started her journey at the age of 8. She will focus on using her success as a public figure to promote her platform for STEAM and literacy. Lauren's plan is to target elementary school students initially. She is a young enthusiast and avid reader with a strong desire to use her skills and influence to help and inspire others to seek out and develop their interest in STEAM and reading. Lauren has raised more than $15,000 in scholarships for young women. Lauren's favorite books are Dork Diaries, A Series of Unfortunate Events and the I Survived book series. This pageant girl believes her success is because of Christ, character, commitment and compassion. Through pageantry she has competed with girls from all over the world, trained with some of the industry's best coaches and has experienced defeat and victory equally. Crown or not, if you leave a pageant calling someone a friend or sister, you won!

What is your favorite quote that can be printed on a T-shirt, written on a mirror or wall?

How to earn a crown:

1. Listen to wise counsel.
2. Obey the Lord our God.
3. Victorious in the battle and at the war.
4. Empower others by being an ideal role model.
5. Servant leader.

What are the 6 major ingredients or components that have contributed to the formulation of your success as a young change-maker thus far?

1. Christ. Philippians 4:13 says, "I can do all things through Christ who strengthens me." I believe, therefore I can achieve.
2. Compassion. My goal is to serve, help and show myself friendly.
3. Character. There is no difference in my attitude whether I win or not.
4. Commitment. The one thing that is significant to trust.
5. Poise. Keeping my posture straight, my head up and my shoulders back is my position for moving forward.
6. Presentation. Your presentation is a result of your preparation. Prepare well.

What does your typical business or work day look like? When do you fit in fun, school, friends and family?

Rise and retreat early. Fortunately, I am able to enjoy all aspects of my life, and that involves family, school, friends and work. All go hand in hand. My family, friends and teachers are able to implement my talent into my education such as preparations, public speaking and presentation. A typical evening sometimes consists of practicing my walk and stage presence in shopping malls and grocery stores. Most of my friends are pageant girls or attend pageants. We go out afterward. My international pageant doubles as a family vacation due to the travel and the length of the pageant. My family, friends and teachers attend my pageants and offer great support. We participate in many of the activities the pageant directors plan throughout the year, like volunteer service projects, tea parties, pajama parties, bowling, photoshoots and ice skating to name a few.

What would you say success means to you? Why is it so important?

I consider myself successful when I accomplish my goals in an ethical and professional manner while helping someone else along the journey.

How important would you say it is to be connected to other young people doing amazing things? How did you make these connections?

It is extremely important to be connected with other young people doing amazing things. It is important to have a posse that

106

believes in and supports you, and you cultivate their visions as well. Proverbs 27:17 says, "As iron sharpens iron, so a man sharpens the countenance of his friend." I always take advantage of moments to tell another girl she is beautiful; her dress is gorgeous and she is doing an awesome job.

How important would you say reading and research is to the success of your business? What 3 business books would you recommend?

Reading and research is a foundation of any business, every dream, and most importantly, the foundation of success. Read, read and read some more!

Marley Dias Gets It Done: And So Can You by Marley Dias, *The Science Behind It: Formulating Success At Any Age* by 26 co-authors and *Rich Dad Poor Dad* by Robert Kiyosaki.

If you could advise a future young mogul to do 3 things before starting their business what would they be?

Always be kind, share and take advantage of every opportunity to encourage another human being! Keep a pen and notepad (journal) next to your bed. My best brainstorming happens in my sleep. Write down every thought, idea and experience you have in reference to your goal. Write down your vision, and the path which you will travel to reach your goal in detail. Be sure to account for detours, potholes and a few jams they are there to build character. Take pictures, they make for an awesome view. Get sponsors, ask for help, invest in yourself too. Donations, mentors and resources are there for you, but you must reach out for them. It's your vision, only you have the key to unlock the door to your success.

What are 3 lessons you have learned so far as a CEO, founder or public figure?

As a public figure, I have learned I am a role model, and to be a good example. You have a responsibility to do the right thing at all times. You will be judged, but only for a moment, let the work you do speak for you. Knowing who you are is the most important trait you can have, and it lasts a lifetime. Lesson three, what God has for you is for you. And yes, He has something for everyone else, too. We all have gifts and talents. Surround yourself with people who will cultivate yours.

Where do you pull inspiration from?

I pull inspiration from my mother and father who continue to push me while also providing me with support to develop my talents. I pull inspiration from the older queens who model great examples of what I can be. The stage and excitement of competition inspires me to be excellent. The opportunity to serve others is the one thing that inspires me to do my best.

What are 3 specific challenges you have had as a young mogul? How have you been able to overcome them?

Procrastination, completing all of my tasks at the last minute. Spending before budgeting and organizing a team with the same goal and visions as myself are my three main challenges. In order to avoid procrastination, I now set small goals and milestones. I gain confidence to stay on task by encouraging myself after each small victory. I now also set a budget and I make sacrifices to keep it. I communicate with people that I work with and make sure it is a win-win situation for everyone.

What are your goals for the future? What's next?

My goals for the future are to attend Spelman College, become Miss Georgia, Miss America, and an obstetrician. Possibly become a pageant coach/advisor, in order to give back everything that has been given to me through my talented coaches. I would love to start a STEAM + Reading Academy in my community, because I have a passion for STEAM and literacy.

I am an official pageant princess, sweetheart and queen. I started my journey at 8 years old. I will focus on using my success as a public figure to promote my platform for STEAM and literacy. My plan is to target elementary school students initially. I am a young enthusiast and avid reader with a strong desire to use my skills and influence to help and inspire others to seek out and develop their interest in STEAM and reading.

ACKNOWLEDGEMENTS

A very special thank you to those who have supported my journey and helped me turn my dreams into a reality...

Mommy; Daddy; CM Sgt Tammy Cleveland; Mikey; Mr. & Mrs. Kylon Harris; Mr. & Mrs. Darrin A. Bettis; Dr. Sonia McKenzie; Ms. Betty Harris; Pastor & Mrs. John F. Hurst; Ms. Shanika N. Jones; Ms. Carmenlita Brown; Mr. & Mrs. Timmy Barker; Mr. & Mrs. Alton Marcus Ms. Lakeia Taylor; Ms. Annie Cleveland; Chief Deputy & Mrs. Eric D. Bryant; Mr. & Mrs. Kelvin Jones; Ms. Keria Smiley; Mr. & Mrs Otis Harris; Ms. Sarah T. Thomas

Chapter XV. An Interview with Zandra
In search of the Perfect Formula

www.zandrabeauty.com
Facebook.com/zandrabeauty
Instagram.com/zandrabeauty
Twitter.com/zandrabeauty
Linkedin.com/zandrabeauty

Like my Co-Authors, I too had to be interviewed. I asked my mom, Tamara Zantell to do the honors. I hope you enjoy and you're encouraged by my answers.

What is your favorite quote that can be printed on a T-shirt, written on a mirror or wall?

I have a few quotes I would like to share with you. I am a huge advocate of affirmations, quotes and manifesting sayings that represent your true self. We may not always have the words that represent how we feel, but we can always find our feelings in the lyrics of songs, pages of a book or written on a wall.

"Change the way you view things, and the things you view will change." I like this quote from my dad because it is realistic. I like golf and I know the toughest shot in golf for many people is a sand shot; however, when I view a sand shot as if I were hitting in the rough (high grass), the sand shot is not difficult and the results are usually favorable.

"Life's most persistent and urgent question is, 'What are you doing for others?'" I really enjoy this quote from Dr. Martin Luther King Jr. We have all been blessed by God in order to bless someone else, and if a person doesn't share their blessing with someone else, that blessing is subject to become a curse.

"You don't have to be great to start but you have to start to be great." One of the things I love about my church is the "come as you are" standard. You don't need to dress fancy or already have a religious background, requirement is that you show up. There are so many examples of how some of the smallest-in-stature people have become some of the greatest people on earth. This quote is all about courage. I am in complete admiration to be in the presence of courageous people. I have received so many compliments and high praise for my accomplishments, but none of them are greater to me than being recognized as courageous.

What would you say the major ingredients or components that have contributed to the formulation of your success as a young change-maker thus far?

There are so many key factors that have played a very important role in the formulation of my success. Considering I started so young, the development of a real formula didn't happen right away. I had to work toward it and learn with every mistake I made. Grit, determination and business acumen and are like muscles; you have to work hard at them in order to grow.

So how do I think success happens? At its core, I think it happens when we acutely break down a problem and come up with an efficient solution. That's it. Success is you finding the answer to someone's problem or unanswered prayer.

1.   **You must work hard.**

This one is first, because in my opinion it's one of the most important.

Unless you're one of the "lucky" ones who wins the lottery, the whole idea of a "get rich quick" process is simply put … not true. Many of us probably watch Shark Tank and read Forbes and see startups earning million-dollar valuations, but the real story is that their "overnight success" was ten years in the making.

Believe me, I know this firsthand. I started my company in 2009, and I didn't start making "real" money until 2016.

When we think about the idea of having a "Millionaire Mindset" we usually think about the cool things like high-powered meetings, making tough decisions that affect employees or maybe even long days and nights.

But the truth is, millionaires aren't afraid to work hard, and they take advantage of the principle of "success begets success." When you have a few small wins, you build on them. You take the next step and you keep stepping until your steps become a run and your run leads you to the top!

The bottom line is hard work, discipline and a willingness to push ahead through any circumstances is the true foundation to all real success.

2.   Your goals need to be crystal clear.

Do you know why millionaires are so willing to work hard? Sure, experiencing regular success helps, but it's also because they have clear goals. They have their goals consistently in plain view so they are clear about what they are working toward on a daily basis.

Let me give you an example. Which of the following statements do you find to be more motivating? "When I start making real money, I'm going to buy a nice car?" or "When I start making real money, I'm buying a white Jeep Wrangler?"

Which one do you think will motivate you more to do the hard work required to become a millionaire?

When I was younger -- when I got my start as a skin care formulator -- I had a picture of the JEEP on my wall and I wrote the exact model I wanted in my dream journey, because that's what I was working toward. My dream was so clear I had already designed the custom plates and could visualize myself walking into the dealership and handing over cash for the truck in full.

That's the kind of goal you need to have if you ever want to be successful. If your current goals are a bit limited or small, now is the time to reevaluate and dream bigger!

3. Accept Failure as a Part of Success

Being afraid of failure makes you overly cautious. If you're constantly afraid of failing, you'll miss out on the opportunities that present themselves to you -- all because you were too scared to move forward. Millionaires take a different approach. Instead of being afraid of failure, they welcome it. They see it for what it is: A chance to learn valuable lessons that show you the way forward.

Sure, you're not going to go out there and deliberately fail. That would be stupid, whether you're an entrepreneur, a penny-stock trader or some other kind of professional. But when you do fail -- and it's virtually guaranteed that you will -- try to learn what you can from the experience. Yes, it'll sting, but if you use your failures as opportunities to improve yourself and your business, you'll eventually become fearless in the face of the smart risks that'll make you a millionaire. When I take on a new endeavor, I try to identify holes. Are there problems in need of solving? What is lacking? Where is there room for improvement? What's missing?

I then assess whether I'm capable of filling those holes. Given what you've learned, how do your weaknesses and strengths match up? Is there an opportunity for you to not only step in, but also excel?

At this point, you may decide you need more information to come to a good conclusion. You might need to take a class or work harder to find a mentor. I am always on the lookout for opportunity. If you want to be successful, you should be, too. It's not enough to want to be successful and commit to working hard. You need to work smart.

4. Put your game plan together.

You have all of the critical information you need to succeed. How are you going to get there? What you need now is a plan of action. Map out how you're going to get from point A to point B. Who are you going to turn to for help? Your road map will inevitably change, but you need a fully fleshed-out framework to turn to when things get chaotic. The quickest path to succeed at anything is by hacking the system -- as Tim Ferriss would say -- first by studying what it is you want to achieve, then by identifying opportunities and finally by crafting a pitch and a plan based on what you learned and your best assets. You never have to reinvent the wheel. Finding your uniqueness-. That's what adds value.

5. Millionaires have successful mentors.

I have to tell you, if I'd had a good mentor when I started trading penny stocks, I'd have been a millionaire years sooner. I was figuring everything out on my own. Learn from my mistake! A good teacher can cut years off your learning curve and save you huge amounts of money. A mentor can't do your work for you, but they can keep you from making the same mistakes they made -- and that's a pretty priceless lesson.

I look at the two millionaire students that have come out of my Millionaire Challenge trading program, and I see that both of them have hit the seven-figure mark in just a few years by leveraging lessons that took me much longer to learn. Their examples prove to me that no matter who you are -- and no matter what you're doing -- you'll benefit from having a successful mentor at your side.

What does your typical business or work day look like?

The daily life of an entrepreneur can be a bit unpredictable. Being a teen CEO adds another layer of crazy on to an already crazy teenage life. Most teens struggle with managing school, a part-time job, household chores, a sport and time with friends. My life is just as crazy as the average teen, but I also have a business to run and employees to manage.

I run a pretty tight ship. My mom taught me that. I understand that my time is extremely valuable, so I don't waste it on meaningless things. I don't spend unnecessary time scrolling the internet, on social media or reading about celebrities. I use that time to enjoy my friends and family. Google Calendar is what I use to manage appointments; I also have project-management software that helps keep everything in one place. Between the two, I know exactly where I am supposed to be, what I should be doing and where I should be at least 3 months in advance. Getting all parts of your business life to work in harmony will never be easy, but it is possible.

What would you say success means to you? Why is it so important?

Success is important because it can be defined differently depending on the person. It helps and motivates me every time I achieve one of my goals; that's success! Whenever I am in front of a room full of girls who are changed, or see things differently because of something I said, that's success! Seeing pictures and watching girls ride to school on a bike that my company purchased, that's success! Creating and building a legacy for my family, that's success! I want to continue to do that!

How important would you say it is to be connected to other young people doing amazing things?

Very important! That's why you are able to read this book. The thing about success is, if you never have the opportunity to see it, touch it, sit next to it or talk to it, you may tend to think it's not possible for you. This makes me sad. There is so much I am committed to; however, sometimes it's lonely being the only one all the time.

How important would you say reading and research is to the success of your business?

To master anything, you first need to study it. What are the rules? Who are the players? What's happened before? Who is successful? Why do people fail? What's considered innovative? You are on a fact-finding mission. Leave no stone unturned. At this stage, I'm just trying to gather information. Because I know the best insight comes from people who have done what I'm trying to do, I try to seek out like-minded people for advice. I ask them to help me understand the topic at hand. A lot of people skip this step. They plunge into new projects with only a cursory understanding of the subject. You might think you're familiar with something, but unless and until you've ruthlessly studied it inside and out, you aren't. There's simply no excuse not to study up! The Internet has made it so easy to do. You may discover the market isn't large enough. Maybe it's headed in a different direction, or has hit its peak. It might be too hard to break into. Either way, you need to know. It's OK to be naïve when you're starting out. In fact, sometimes having a fresh perspective can be helpful, but if you don't take the time to understand what the challenges ahead are going to be at the very beginning, you will experience pain later on. I know, because it's happened to me.

If you could advise a future young mogul to do 3 things before starting their business what would that be?

Plan to sacrifice, research, and prepare to be lucky.

- Plan to sacrifice - When I began my business, I was only 9 years old; therefore, planning to sacrifice wasn't too high on my priority list. However, when I began to take my business seriously, I realized that I cannot be everywhere all the time. As a business owner, I had to learn on the fly about sacrifice. I had to learn how to sacrifice my personal wants in order to have business success. This initially was a big challenge for me, but eventually I conceded to the need to sacrifice. There were plenty of times in which I had to tell my friends "no" to going to the movies, going to parties or simply hanging out; there were instances in which my friends really believed I was brushing them off callously. I had to correct them, I am not brushing them off callously or capriciously, but rather initially or sacrificially for the betterment of my business. Eventually, some of my friends began to understand and agreed to plan our time together around my schedule or in advance. However, there were some people who cut me off entirely; including some I liked very much. But, I have learned people are in our lives for two reasons; either they are in our lives for a season, to eventually fall off, or they are in our lives for a reason; to sacrifice with you. Either way, I am thankful for their presence.

- Research - There is nothing more important than being able to communicate articulately, intelligently and respectfully about your business and industry. I didn't truly grasp this concept until I applied for admission into the University of Buffalo School of Business Center for Entrepreneurial Leadership program. During the interview, the interviewer asked a bunch of detailed questions; ones that represented distinct knowledge. The interviewed asked my mom the questions, but I answered them. After a few questions -- asked and answered by me -- the interviewer asked, surprised, "Whose business is this?" I answered confidently, "This is my business." Although I was too young to participate - participation required an age of 18 -- impressed with my knowledge of the industry, the interviewer presented my case to the head dean for the school of management in an effort to have me accepted. I was accepted, and I credited to my relentless researching habit. I will never forget my dad telling me about the researching habit of the Secretary of Defense under the Kennedy Administration, Robert S. McNamara. Secretary McNamara, according to my dad, would spend 3 hours a day per subject for one meeting with President Kennedy and/or other administration officials. I take a similar approach

116

when I engage into my research, and I encourage other to do the same.

- Prepare to be lucky - Working hard isn't enough. The most successful businesses have been in receipt of some luck; including my business. However, luck just doesn't happen to just anyone, luck happens to those who are prepared for it. For example, winning the lottery is luck; however, the preparation for that luck requires the purchase of a lottery ticket. No one wins the lottery without the purchase of the winning ticket. There is a catch phrase my dad uses while coaching, "You gotta shoot to miss." I admit, I didn't understand the true meaning off this, I suspect his team didn't understand it entirely, either. When my dad explained the phrase, I completely understood, and the phrase should be taken literally. This is a form of preparing to be lucky. If your team is down by 1 and you have the ball, but you don't shoot, the team is guaranteed to lose. However, if you take the shot, no matter the difficulty of the shot, you could get lucky and make the basket and win the game for your team. The preparation in this example is taking shots during practice or at home. If you don't prepare for luck, you will get stuck holding the ball at the end.

What are lessons you have learned so far as a CEO, Founder or Public Figure?

It's okay to make mistakes, meeting others and making connections are very important and are crucial sometimes in making or breaking your brand, faith. Having a support system is important, however, sometimes you have to create your own.

Where do you pull inspiration from?

I pull my inspiration from my desire to help girls like me. I have had so many really tough days. Let downs galore, but you know what? My worst days are still better than another girl's best day somewhere else in the world. That thought motivates me, it keeps me focused on the change I wish to create. I have a huge vision and idea of what I want to see happen in this world. It's written on my walls, written in this book and written in my heart. That vision keeps me going every single day.

In addition, my family is a huge driving force for me. They are my support system, and I work hard to make them proud.

When I was 9 years old, I received inspiration from my dad to become independent and control my destiny. I have an unusual passion to use lip balm for as long as I can remember. I recall one day at the age of 9, I asked my dad to buy me a lip balm. This was par for the course, because for years he offered no objection to this daily request. On this particular day, I asked him what I have been asking him for years; "Dad, will you buy me a new lip balm?" Anticipating the answer to be the usual answer yes, his reply was, "No! I am not buying you any more lip balm! Why don't you just make your own?" I recall feeling like this was no big deal; in fact I felt a bit privileged, because dad just gave me permission to explore. It's a bit ironic that I felt this way, because dad used to always provide me and my siblings his favorites stanzas and the one that came into my mind at the time was the one from T.S. Eliot's Little Gidding:

> *We shall not cease from exploration*
> *And the end of all our exploring*
> *Will be to arrive where we started*
> *And know the place for the first time.*

Every time my dad spoke this stanza, I only understood the first line: *We shall not cease from exploration*. I didn't realize it at the time, but I am a dreamer. I dream big, so much so, I don't believe anything is impossible. This is likely the reason; my dad's NO was instantly translated into New Option. I began to brainstorm how to create lip balm. I was fascinated with the option to have YouTube videos as a guideline to my explorations. I continued my explorations by creating my lip balm recipe. Two months after being rejected by my dad, I had a finished lip balm product. I was so excited to share my lip balm with everyone. I was sanguine everyone was going to love it, too. I passed it around my grandfather's church to any parishioner I could find, until one of the parishioners went into her purse and gave me a dollar for my lip balm. The largess from the parishioner was rocket fuel on an already burning desire to explore. I had explored with my creativity for more than 5 years. Shortly after my 13th birthday and my graduation from the University at Buffalo School of Management Entrepreneurship Leadership Program, I ended my exploration and rebranded my business; returning to the place in which I started and knowing that place, for the very first time.

118

Today I am viewed as a successful teenage entrepreneur by many people. In fact, last year, I won the 2017 Small Business Administration Teenpreneur of the year. I have successfully negotiated major retail partnerships with Paper Source, Whole Foods Market, American Eagle, COSTCO and Wegmans. The milestones I have reached with my business have opened up many doors to some of the world largest businesses, such as Nike, Twitter and Uber. I am proud of my business accomplishments, but I am defined by something greater. When I was 13, I watched a movie that changed my life forever. The movie was called Girl Rising. The movie was about girls across the world being denied the rights many of us take for granted: the right to an education. Not only were these girls denied this basic right, they were also put into slavery and forced to marry and have children. At that moment, I knew I had to make a difference. I converted my business into a vehicle for change and in order to help these girls, I was prepared to drive it until the wheels fell off. I decided to become a girls' rights advocate and use my business platform to reach and inspire as many girls as possible. I donate up to 10 % of my business net profits to girls' education. I was so inspired, I challenged myself to do a Ted Talk about how girls across the world were being treated. I became an ambassador for International Day of The Girl Movement. In my community of Buffalo, N.Y., I hosted a free event for girls. The event introduced girls to successful women who provided workshops on how they conquered their own obstacles as young girls. The event provided workshops that included S.T.E.A.M sessions, life lessons, etiquette and more. The success of this event has allowed it to receive a proclamation from the Mayor of Buffalo declaring every Oct. 11, "Day of The Girl Buffalo." This past October was our fifth year and we had more than 500 girls! There is no greater feeling for me than to believe, because of my presence and passion to help, some girl(s) have acquired the inspiration to become liberated. I personally know what it means to be liberated. I started my natural skin care business when I was 9 years old. After buying me lip balm every day, my dad one day told me "No." He also told me, sarcastically, that I should make my own. I wasn't upset at all; in fact, I was encouraged. Prior to this "no" from my dad, he would always say to me and my siblings, "Change the way you view things, and the things you view will change." I took his no, not as he intended it, but as I needed it to be -- Next Option. This is the exact message I endeavor to send to my audience every time I am invited to speak at conferences across the nation. I want them to know, being a change agent isn't easy, or popular, but if we allow the greater good to be a guideline for ourselves, we can really do something special for this world and each other. Recently, I was a keynote speaker at a conference in Kansas City, Mo. There were about 100 underprivileged girls in the audience. I spoke to them for about 40 minutes, telling them about my business and my overall story. I have been traveling and speaking across the country for years, but there was something a bit different about this audience. When I completed my speech and hosted a workshop -- teaching them how to make their own natural skin care products, at the conclusion of the event, something special happened. I was reintroduced to give closing remarks and one of the girls raised her hand to ask me a question. She asked me as she smiled in bemusement, "If running a business is so hard and you have sacrificed so much, then why are you so happy to keep doing it?" I responded without hesitation, "Because my presence inspires you to smile and feel confident to ask me this question; that's how it begins."

What is one of your biggest challenges you have had as a young mogul? How have you been able to overcome them?

I faced many challenges in the earlier stages of my company and of course tons throughout my journey. Not being taken seriously, being the only one, balancing life ...

One of my favorite but most exhausting challenges occurred when I re-branded my business. I started my natural skin care company at 9 years old. I named my company Azariah's Innocence; Azariah is my middle name and the Innocence part of the name relates to the quiddity of me and my products. My packaging was on plain brown paper with a colorful logo of an African-American woman in a bathtub. At the time, I thought it was great. However, when I was enrolled into the University at Buffalo School of Business Entrepreneurship Course at 13, I realized my packaging wasn't going to get me where I wanted to be; i.e. in stores. Therefore, April 2014, I began to change everything; starting with my business name. I changed the business name from Azariah's Innocence to Zandra. I spent the next 4 months with a skilled branding expert to change my packaging. I changed the logo to my signature, I included a unique inspirational quote on every product package I offered; 78 total. All product scents had matching packaging. For example, my Lemon Tea Tree scent comes in a lemon/yellow-colored package. By the end of November 2014, I was ready to officially launch my rebranded business. The results were more auspicious than I thought. I started getting multiple wholesale inquiries from small businesses, but no major retailers. However, I had gross sales over $50,000. In July 2016, my business was selected by Etsy to participate in the Etsy Open Call Competition. The Etsy Open Call Competition is an opportunity for small businesses to pitch their business to major retail companies such as: Macy's, Wholefood, Paper Source and more in hopes of landing a purchasing order – or a Golden PO as Etsy referred to them. My business was one of 36 selected out of Etsy's small business pool of thousands. Being more determined than nervous, I confidently pitched my business to all of the major retailers. I wasn't able to tell which of the buyers liked my products or not, but every one of them said they liked my packaging. At the end of the business pitch, all vendors met in a large room to learn their fate: If they wowed the buyers enough to get the Golden PO. I was so nervous as I listened to six businesses hear their name called. With only a few more Golden POs remaining, I remained sanguine. Paper Source, a stationery company, stood up and said how impressed they were with a particular vendor and how in much in awe they were that this vendor was able to do what they had done at such a young age (I was the youngest competitor ever). They announced their Golden PO went to Zandra! The place erupted with so much excitement and many cheers. I was so overwhelmed with emotion. It took 2 years after my rebrand to achieve the goal that eluded me far too long. Paper Source had my products in all of their 122 stores across the nation. As of now, my products are sold in multiple major retail stores such as American Eagle, Whole Foods Market, Wegmans and COSTCO. I am currently in negotiations with Bed Bath & Beyond for a 2018 launch.

I am Zandra A. Cunningham, I turned my kitchen table hobby into an international brand. My mission is to educate and empower girls and women across the globe via STEAM and entrepreneurial opportunities. I am committed to using my platform to help my community and other young moguls develop and grow their dreams into action. As a girls education advocate, I will always work toward supporting, inspiring and connection girls to the resources they need to not only survive but to thrive!

ACKNOWLEDGEMENTS

A very special thank you to those who have supported my journey and helped me turn my dreams into a reality...

My Miracle Missions Full Gospel Church family; Mayor Byron Brown; The Foundry Buffalo; The University At Buffalo School of Management; Ms. Katia Soldatenko, The Administration and Staff of Erie County Medical Center; Ms. Vanessa S. Turner; Ms. Cekeita Murdaugh; Ms. Catherine Roberts; The West Side Bazaar; Ms. Michelle Barron; my superstar makeup artist and family Ms. Keyonna Willis; Ms. Detra M. Trueheart; Ms. Yanik Jenkins; My Women In The Spotlight Goinglobal Family; Francesca Mesiah; Ms. Tosha Groves; Ms. Dechantell Lloyd; Ms. Brittni Smallwood; Ms. Christina Lopez; Dr. Ruben West; Ms. Lauren Millian; My NAWBO Buffalo-Niagara family; The McNally Family; My awesome Thomas/Lewis/ Cunningham/Clarke "TLC" Family!

Chapter XVI. No Dream is too BIG
Olivia Grinston

www.oliviareneeinspires.com
Facebook.com/OliviaReneeInspires
Twitter.com/OliviaRenee

Olivia Grinston is an 8-year-old third grader from Collinsville, Ill. She is full of life and ambition. Olivia is a mini mogul making moves in her community and inspiring other youth. Olivia is the owner of Joyful Jewels Boutique, an online boutique featuring the latest fashion trends and accessories for young girls. Joyful Jewels was birthed out of of her desire to inspire young girls around the world to be their best selves! And to never let anyone steal your joy! Olivia loves the little details and wants all little divas to shop her online house of fashion. From custom bracelets to fashionable apparel, Joyful Jewels has you covered! Olivia is also a youth speaker and motivator and upcoming author. She has a passion for inspiring other young people to be their best selves. Olivia has a knack for details, and is a natural-born leader. She is taking the world by storm and is ready to encourage future generations of leaders and entrepreneurs.

Olivia was recently awarded and recognized for her young entrepreneurship by the BLACK Tie Community Award committee for being young entrepreneurship. This was a major opportunity for Olivia.

M.A.D.E Moguls is a youth entrepreneurship program that works with students ages 11-17 from primarily low-income households in the St. Louis metropolitan area. This program uses entrepreneurship as a platform to help build character and develop valuable transferable life skills. Developed under the mantra "Be Inspired. Be Great. Be You!" M.A.D.E. created a curriculum and program that is both culturally relevant and educational.

This organization recognized Olivia for her work in the community and for being an inspirational young entrepreneur.

Olivia is excited to be walking in her purpose and being a positive role model for her peers to look up to.

What is your favorite quote that can be printed on a T-shirt, written on a mirror or wall?

My favorite quote is, "No one can steal my joy," by Olivia Grinston.

What are the 6 major ingredients or components that have contributed to the formulation of your success as a young change-maker thus far?

Number one is God. My faith and belief in God keep me going. Without God, I wouldn't be here, and I would not have purpose. I pray over my ideas and passion daily in order to keep everything in perspective, and to ask for wisdom and direction. Number two, learning to have fun. I have learned not to take myself too seriously. Life is to be enjoyed. Mistakes will happen, and that's OK, I can learn from them and move on. I learned to enjoy every moment of my journey and inspire others along the way. Number three, a strong support system. My parents and grandparents are my biggest supporters. They constantly pray for me and encourage me to chase my dreams. It is so important to have family you can lean on and learn from. Number four, believing in myself. Aside from having a great support system, I have to want success for myself. I have to believe that I can do anything and have my dreams and desires. If you don't even believe in yourself, it's hard to learn and grow. If you believe, you can, you can! Number five, understanding brand. To broaden my business, I have grown to learn that everything I do is a representation of my brand. This is so important because as I go through my day-to-day, I want to make sure my actions and language reflect my brand. Number six, having patience. A lot of times, I want things to happen right away, but I am learning to have patience. Success doesn't just happen overnight. You have to work really hard and learn there are going to be ups and downs. You have to have patience and stick with your vision.

What does your typical business or work day look like? When do you fit in fun, school, friends and family?

I work with my mom on putting together a schedule for the week. We spend time scheduling our social media posts, making inspirational videos and putting together looks for our customers. We make sure we factor in time for fun and family. The best part about my business is that I get to work with my family.

What would you say success means to you? Why is it so important?

Success is doing what you love to do while inspiring others. It's important, because we are all here for a purpose. And it's important to find that purpose and be great.

How important would you say it is to be connected to other young people doing amazing things? How did you make these connections?

It's important to be connected to other young entrepreneurs because we can all encourage one another and be the light and inspiration for generations to come.

How important would you say reading and research is to the success of your business? What 3 business books would you recommend?

Reading and doing research is very important to the success of any business. First, I will always read the Bible. That is where you get your strength, wisdom and encouragement.

Three books I would recommend:

1. ***How to Turn $100 into $1,000,000 Earn! Save! Invest!*** by James McKenna
3. ***The Everything Kids' Money Book*** by Brette McWhorter Sember, J.D.
4. ***The Totally Awesome Business Book for Kids*** by several authors
If you could advise a future young mogul to do 3 things before starting their business what would they be?

1. Listen to the advice of those wiser than you
2. Know that you don't know it all.
3. Be patient.

What are 3 lessons you have learned so far as a CEO, founder or public figure?

1. One, be disciplined.
2. Two, no one else will run my business for you.
3. Three, your actions speak for your brand.

Where do you pull inspiration from?

I pull my inspiration from my mom. She works so hard. She manages several businesses while still being there for our family. She inspires me to be the best me possible.

What are 3 specific challenges you have had as a young mogul? How have you been able to overcome them?

One, balancing school, work and fun. I was able to overcome this challenge by listening to the advice of my mother and creating a schedule for myself.

Two, learning that I am my brand and everything I do reflects that. What I do or say are all reflections of my brand.

Three, staying focused. Sometimes, I can be easily distracted by the things going on around me. And I have to remind myself that my visions and goals are not going to work themselves. So, it's important for me to stay on track and not lose focus.

What are your goals for the future? What's next?

My goals for the future are to continue to grow my brand, Joyful Jewels Boutique and Olivia Renee Inspires. I want to continue speaking to youth and motivating them to be all that they can be. No matter their situation. No matter there circumstance They are beautiful and wonderfully made with a divine purpose.

I am an author and entrepreneur, I started my business at 8 years old. My mission is to inspire young girls see their potential and to let them know they have purpose and to never let anyone steal their joy! In my business I help girls ages 6 to 12 to aim high in every area of their life. No age is too young to start realizing your potential. I hope to be able to work with you and inspire you to be the best you possible!

ACKNOWLEDGEMENTS

A very special thank you to those who have supported my journey and helped me turn my dreams into a reality...

Phillip & Christine St.Vil; Fidelia Namirembe; Don and Tanya Barnett; Heather Parsons; Michael St.Vil; Mary Kiganda; Eric Kareem; Kimberly McKissick; Pastors Charles & Cynthia Williams; Keianna Johnson; Laila & Maya Cole; Nevaeh & Christian Skeeter; Cal and Renee Coakley; Shantae, Kennedy & Mikayla Pelt; Shanise N. Griffith; Sherrill Mosee; Tara Darnley; Nourah Shuaibi; Marlene St.Vil; George & Agnes Kiganda

Chapter XVII. Two Sisters Running A Sweet Business
Layla & Mya Parish

www.sugabbeauty.com
Facebook.com/sugababesbeauty
Instagram.com/sugababesbeauty

Layla and Mya Parish are two sisters running a sweet business! When Layla and Mya started their business, Suga Babes Beauty, April 2012, they had one idea; to sell sugar scrubs. Little did they know their idea would turn into something more than they could have ever imagined. The heartbeat of Suga Babes Beauty is their amazing plant-based bath and body products, and innovative skincare workshops for girls and teens.

Layla and Mya have not only grown with their business, they have actually grown into their business. They are the creators, innovators and driving forces behind their brand. They are constantly thinking of new ideas and ways to implement them. Who are these two sisters running this sweet business? Glad you asked ...

Layla, now a 16-year-old confident high schooler, has not always been the teen you see today. As a little girl, Layla loved looking and posing in the mirror, pretending to be a model. She thought she was beautiful. Then, those thoughts were shattered by the views of society and how media portrayed the perfect look. She was consumed with losing weight and finding clothing that would hide her unwanted shape. For the longest time, she struggled with her insecurities and never told anyone. She did some soul-searching, developed an intimate relationship with God and her eyes were opened. She realized she was, in fact, fearfully and wonderfully made. Her worth was not defined by society. She realized that she was in fact worthy and enough. She was no longer insecure. Layla made a vow to herself and God that she would use her company as a platform to help other girls realize their true purpose and beauty.

Mya, an 12-year-old middle schooler, is full of spunk and pizzazz! Mya has two driving forces of motivation. One is to share her journey with other young teens. Her message is very clear: "You are never too young to start living your dreams." She can totally see the big picture for Suga Babes Beauty -- International all the way. Second is to continue to increase awareness and the impact of bullying. Mya knows all too well about bullying. She was bullied. She overcame what was happening to her and took back her power.

Layla and Mya have been blessed with many opportunities to share their journey. They have been featured on the front page of the business section in the Houston Chronicle, appeared in an article in the Wall Street Journal and appeared on Fox 26 News Houston and Good Day Sacramento. They were keynote speakers at Dell Computers in Round Rock, Tex., panelists at the Kids Expo in Sacramento, Calif. and they have been featured in numerous online publications and blogs. Layla and Mya are exceptional students. Layla maintains a 3.9 gpa, is a member of the National Honor Society, and a member of other leadership clubs. Mya is a honor roll student, cheerleader for her school, and involved in various clubs. They are highly involved in their community and believe in serving others. Their mission is to inspire teens around the world by continuing to build their brand, host workshops and speak on topics that are relevant to youth today.

What is your favorite quote that can be printed on a T-shirt, written on a mirror or wall?

You are more powerful than you know. you are beautiful just as you are. -Melissa Etheridge.

What are the 6 major ingredients or components that have contributed to the formulation of your success as a young change-maker thus far?

When operating a business you must have a path or plan in order for your business to be successful. When we first started we really

129

did not understand this process because we were just 5 and 10 years old, so of course our mother helped us out. Now that we are older and we have grown with and into our business, we understand the importance of a plan and the major ingredients of having a successful business. There are different stages of development that requires work and preparation. Six major ingredients that have contributed to our success were:

1. **Brainstorming.** Brainstorming is key. Is your idea a good fit for you? You may have a great idea for a business, however, it may not be the best fit for you. As you are brainstorming ask yourself these questions. What am I passionate about? What purpose will this new venture serve? Will it bring solutions? What are my strengths and weaknesses? To find out your strengths and weaknesses take the SWOT Analysis. The SWOT Analysis is a strategic planning technique used to help you identify your *strengths*, *weaknesses*, *opportunities* and *threats* related to business. This is a great assessment to take. We did not take this assessment when we first started, however we did when we got older and it really helped us to map our business better.

2. **Planning and preparation.** You must create a plan. Within your plan, you must clearly identify your business's goals and mission otherwise you will be all over the place. Research your audience. Who will you target? How much will this new business cost? Create a spreadsheet with the cost and/or estimated cost of items that will be needed for your new business.

3. **Understand your customers.** It is important to know your customers. You want to produce a product that is usable and needed. You customers will determine your failure or success.

4. **Execution.** Staying focused on your goal is critical.

5. **Stay the course.** Never quit. Never abort your mission. Trust the process and be patient.

6. **Drive.** Determination is everything. Persistence and determination are omnipotent. Steve Jobs once stated, "I'm convinced that about half of what separates the successful entrepreneurs from the non-successful ones is pure perseverance".

What does your typical business or work day look like? When do you fit in fun, school, friends and family?

Of course we are full-time students with a pretty heavy school workload, therefore we have a schedule that we try our best to live by. We try to fit in at least one hour per day to work on our business during the week. Our weekends are pretty busy hosting mobile spa parties and skincare workshops. When we have parties and/or workshops on the weekends, we spend about 6 hours working on a Saturday. We also do pop-up shops on the weekends we don't host parties. There are some sacrifices when it comes to spending time with our family/friends when we have events on the weekends, however, our mom makes certain that we still have balance.

What would you say success means to you? Why is it so important?

Success means different things to different people. For us, success doesn't mean we have a lot of money in the bank. Success means serving others, making a difference in someone's life and having a well-rounded life both naturally and spiritually. Being successful in life is very important to us because it means that we are leaving footprints for others to follow.

How important would you say it is to be connected to other young people doing amazing things? How did you make these connections?

Being connected to other young people doing amazing things is very important. There is a saying, "iron sharpens iron" and that is so true. When we are around other young people doing amazing things we get a charge! We are motivated and inspired. Our creative juices get flowing and collaborations are created. We meet these amazing young people at events we attend, social media, and believe it or not just in casual conversation when we are out and about. One time we were at a store shopping and started talking to someone who was a young mogul like us! It was exciting to hear their journey.

How important would you say reading and research is to the success of your business? What 3 business books would you recommend?

Reading and research is key to the success of our business. Reading and research broadens our horizons and stirs your train of thoughts. It expands our verbal intelligence so that we can effectively articulate ourselves and inspire others. There is power in reading and research. It can transform your business. It transformed our business. When we first started our business, we did not know anything about the personal care industry. Through reading, research and attending classes, we learned a lot about running a business and the personal care industry.

Three books we would recommend are:

1. **Just Blow it Up: Firepower for Living an Unlimited Life** by Dixie Gillaspie
2. **Growing a Business** by Paul Hawken
3. **Seven Habits of Highly Effective People** by Stephen R. Covey

If you could advise a future young mogul to do 3 things before starting their business what would they be?

Our advice would be to find something that you love to do, like a hobby that you're passionate about; research the kind of business that you want to get into, know the industry, write the vision and make it plain. And if we could add one more it would be to find a mentor or someone who can help guide you along the way.

What are 3 lessons you have learned so far as a CEO, founder or public figure?

1. Listening to our customers: Being willing to change
2. Cost-effective marketing: Time is money
3. Stay focused: Don't get distracted by the noise

Where do you pull inspiration from?

Our inspiration comes from our mother who is our No. 1 supporter. We also draw inspiration from other young moguls, industry leaders such as personal care influencers, and beauty and fashion bloggers/influencers.

What are 3 specific challenges you have had as a young mogul? How have you been able to overcome them?

When we started our business, we were excited and it was a huge achievement for us especially at such a young age, however there were some challenges. Some specific challenges for us were:

132

1. Capital, money
2. Building our customer base, exposure
3. Time management

In order to overcome challenges, you must develop a plan. We created a challenge journal. In this journal we wrote down the challenges we faced in our business and how we would overcome them. We created a timeline and worked toward each challenge. We realized that writing things down is one of the most important things you can do in your business. When you write things down, they come to life and you can see things clearer.

What are your goals for the future? What's next?

Our mission is to be the premier vegan bath and body product line for teens that will enhance your well-being organically. To be known for inspiring teen girls on the importance of taking care of their skin by offering fun, innovative, and interactive skincare workshops. To promote being kind to your skin and the environment.

We will continue to build and expand our brand. Suga Babes Beauty will be an international and household name when it comes to teen bath and body products. Within the next five years we will have a standalone boutique that will be a one-of-a-kind -- we can't spill the beans yet, it's still in the works. Just know that no one in the world will have this concept. Our goal is to not only be trendsetters but a legacy builders, leaving footprints of success everywhere we tread.

We are Suga Architects, we started our business when we were 5 and 10 years of age. Our mission is to be the premier vegan bath and body product line for teens that will enhance your well-being organically. To be known for inspiring teen girls on the importance of taking care of their skin by offering fun, innovative and interactive skincare workshops. To promote being kind to your skin and the environment. We are determined to share the importance of healthy skincare to other teen girls. Our skin is the largest organ on our body, therefore we must be intentional on what we put on it and how we take care of it.

We are dreamers, risk takers, creators, experts in our industry and the generation that will take personal skincare to the next level. We hope to be able to work with you and help you understand the importance of taking care of your skin organically.

ACKNOWLEDGEMENTS

A very special thank you to those who have supported my journey and helped me turn my dreams into a reality...

Jacquie B.; Robert and Carolyn Burrell, Sr.; Robert and Deidre Burrell, Jr.; Sedric and Angela Burrell; Christopher Burrell; Brianne Burrell; Nathian and Brenda Chandler; Mike and Jenny Perry; Josh and Delianna Burrell; Helena Washington; Jonathan and Amir Burrell; Treyvian Webb; Kendra Calvin; Andrea Allen; Kyndall Rosenthal; Gene and Gail Johnson; Tanisha Hall; Carmisha Davis; Maria Howell; Tonya and Anetria Kerr; Angela, Zoe and Crystal Johnson; Shakeira aka "Kiwi" Woods; Joanna Moore; Kathy and Mason Partak; Kyle and Grace Moffett; James and Shermel Parish

Chapter XVIII. Becoming a Beauty Boss

Zhanyia McCullough

www.ZhanyiaInspires.me
Facebook.com/ZhanyiaInspires
Instagram.com/Zhanyiainspires
Twitter.com/zhanyiainspires

At the young age of 12, Zhanyia McCullough is already proving to be a bundle of talent! Born in Atlanta, Ga., and raised in Roosevelt, NY since the age of two. Zhanyia is a creator at heart with a passion for the arts and sciences. Her favorite hobbies include writing, dancing, cheerleading and spending time with friends and family. And, unlike most other 12-year-olds, she has already invested her future into developing a career as a full-fledged entrepreneur and beauty chemist in training!

Her business, Zhanyia Inspires, combines her love of beauty and science. Zhanyia and her team created the business idea at Teen Entrepreneur Camp in Freeport, NY. Her team overcame the competition and won the Shark Tank event for "Most Profitable" and "Best Pitch." Starting from this significant moment in her life, Zhanyia started her first business selling lip balms and lip scrubs. More products, including a hair growth oil, are in the works. In the future, she plans to create Beauty Science STEM Kits for those who want to make their own beauty products.

Zhanyia's success isn't just in her entrepreneurial skills. She is smart, dedicated, confident and curious about the world around her. She graduated from Centennial Avenue Elementary School as the salutatorian of her class. Currently in middle school, she is on the Dean's List and High Honor Roll. As for her extracurricular life, she has taken part in five productions at Gloria Eve School of the Arts, and had the honor of auditioning for Debbie Allen Dance Company in New York City.

Today, Zhanyia continues to develop her business. She hopes to inspire and teach girls that they have what it takes to make something truly exceptional for themselves. It's all about finding inner beauty, building confidence and creating healthy self-esteem in the face of adversity.

What is your favorite quote that can be printed on a T-shirt, written on a mirror or wall?

If I have to print my favorite quote on a tee, mirror or wall, I'll put an acrostic poem that spells out LIT, "leader in training." I feel everyone has the ability to become a leader.

What are the 6 major ingredients or components that have contributed to the formulation of your success as a young change-maker thus far?

One component is networking with other young entrepreneurs. Another is my prior knowledge that I learned from past marketing and other related events. Another is my reputation as an outgoing person. Another is my hard work and drive. Another is my participation in a young entrepreneurship camp during the summer, I really enjoyed being around like-minded kids. Lastly, me being salutatorian in sixth grade. Accomplishing that goal showed me that hard work pays off.

What does your typical business or work day look like? When do you fit in fun, school, friends and family?

A typical work day for me is to get up around 6am to get ready for school. I attend a charter school, so I have a extended day, so I may not reach home until after 4 p.m. From 4-6 I may have after-school activities like dance and cheerleading. Once I finish my homework, I go online and do my research. I take some notes and sometimes even watch other webinars. My formulating days are usually on the weekends. mainly on Sundays. I try to keep Saturdays for my friends and family, but sometimes I may have to "work.".

136

What would you say success means to you? Why is it so important?

To me success is when you are proud of yourself, and your accomplishments. And it is important that you define success for yourself, how can others define your success? It's doing what you love, while still helping and inspiring others.

How important would you say it is to be connected to other young people doing amazing things? How did you make these connections?

It is important to be connected with other young entrepreneurs doing amazing things because you can learn a thing or two, and it can also help with your social skills. It allows you to see what is possible. I use that as my inspiration. You can connect by networking on social media. I get involved in young entrepreneurs' clubs and camps. Whenever possible, I will attend events where I know there will be other young entrepreneurs.

How important would you say reading and research is to the success of your business? What 3 business books would you recommended?

It is mandatory that you read and research in the process of starting a business.

I would recommend *Kidpreneurs: Young Entrepreneurs with Big Ideas!* by Adam and Matthew Toren, *The Making of a Young Entrepreneur: A Kid's Guide to Developing a Mindset for Success* by Gabrielle Jordan, *7 Habits of Highly Effective Teens* by Sean Covey and a bonus, of course, The Science Behind It series.

If you could advise a future young mogul to do 3 things before starting their business what would they be?

I would advise a future young mogul to do their research, connect with other young entrepreneurs and to get one of the books I recommended and read it before starting their own business.

What are 3 lessons you have learned so far as a CEO, founder or public figure?

I learned to start small and think big. Also, I learned that every step you take, you're getting closer to your dreams. In addition, I learned that there is always room for improvement.

Where do you pull inspiration from?

I pull inspiration from places and other people. My Godmother, Shonda, inspires me. She is a hairstylist and I love everything about hair.

What are 3 specific challenges you have had as a young mogul? How have you been able to overcome them?

One challenge is my frustration when I don't know how to answer a question. Another challenge is my busy schedule. Sometimes I don't have time to hang out with my friends or attend parties. I just keep telling myself it will all pay off, so I keep going. Another challenge is self-confidence and me being able to do it all. Sometimes I allow the fact that I am only 12 stop me, or should I say, slow me down. But then I have my mom tell me to use that to my advantage. I overcame my challenges by believing in myself and by accommodating my work schedule.

One day I watched some videos from a young girl on Instagram (I forgot her name) and she was talking about how she did it all herself, so another way I have been able to overcome most of my challenges is that I actually did research and watched YouTube videos, or videos of other people doing it, and I learn from them.

What are your goals for the future? What's next?

My goal is to make more than $24,000 to invest in the business and toward other things regarding young entrepreneurs. I want to continue to formulate hair products until I have a full line (shampoo, conditioner, gel, hair masks and edge control (my edges are important, too). I also would like to inspire other girls and let them know that science can be fun when you learn to create products that we already love; Beauty products!

I am a Zhanyia McCullough, CEO of Zhanyia Inspires, and I started my business at 11 years old.My mission is to help young girls learn about the "Beauty of Science". In my business, I formulate beauty products for my family's beauty brand and I also help girls ages 9-18 to embrace STEAM (Science, Technology, Engineering, Arts and Math) buy teaching them how to formulate beauty products. I also am a high honor roll student, dancer, cheerleader,speaker and I love all things hair!. I hope to be able to work with you and help to teach you all about the "Beauty of Science".

ACKNOWLEDGEMENTS

A very special thank you to those who have supported my journey and helped me turn my dreams into a reality...

Chanel McCullough; James McCullough; Zhakeirah Ephraim; Zhakyia Epraim; Shamira Ephraim; Debra Brisco; Sharaine Felder; Deboni Felder; Lisa McMillian; Dawn McMillian; LaShonda Brown; Runeail Brown; Arjla Harris; Kenneth Harris; Omari Harris; Stephen Fox; Ellashia Spaulding; Darryl Wilson; Teneisha Peets; Charles Castillo

Chapter XIX. Mastering the 3 "B's" Beauty, Brains and Business Owner
Gabrielle Williams

www.gloriouspastriesbygabrielle.com
Facebook.com/gloriouspastries1
Instagram.com/gloriouspastries1

Gabrielle was born in Georgia but currently resides in Maryland. Her love for baking presented itself at an early age. Upon entering a new school, she bullied by her fellow classmates. The stress of the bullying began to effect on her self-esteem and confidence. As a way to deal with her feelings, she took to the kitchen and, found comfort through baking. In August 2013, after meeting Gabrielle Jordan, entrepreneur, motivational speaker and author of *The Making of a Young Entrepreneur* she found encouragement in the older Gabrielle's words to "Dream Big." It was at that moment, Gabrielle started her own business at the age of 9, and Glorious Pastries by Gabrielle was introduced to the world.

Based on Gabrielle's entrepreneurial spirit, in 2016, Jim Coleman, Prince George County Economic Development Corporation President & CEO, implemented the county's first ever "Kidpreneur Day." She was selected to be the Vice Chairman of this youth event, working closely with the Economic Development Corporation and County Executive's office. The event drew more 100 aspiring kid/teen entrepreneurs.

Gabrielle's success has gained her local, national and international recognition. She has been featured in the Washington Post, Washington Informer, ABC's The Chew, Voices of America, Woman's World Magazine and numerous local media networks. Notable people Gabrielle has had the opportunity to meet include state senators/representatives, 2016 Miss Virginia USA Desiree Williams, 2016 Miss Maryland World America Tarese Taylor, celebrity chef Chef Huda, NFL's Washington Redskins players, gospel recording artists Kirk Franklin, Tye Tribbett, Jonathan McReynolds, just to name a few. Her most cherished moments were baking for 1975 Tony Award winning choreographer George Faison and having Emmy Award winning makeup artist Reggie Wells (former makeup artist to Oprah Winfrey) taste several of her desserts. Her dream is to become a celebrity pastry chef.

When not baking, she speaks to youth and adults about the effects of bullying/cyberbullying and how they can overcome the stress. She likes to read, play the drums, and compete in beauty pageants (having been crowned 2017 Miss Pre-Teen DELMARVA Miss America Co-Ed (MAC) Pageant and 2017 Jr. Teen Miss DELMARVA). She holds a First-Degree Black Belt in Tae Kwon Do and First Gup (Red Belt) in Tang Soo Do. She's a three-time AAU National Champion in Sparring and has won numerous state/regional championships in the states of Maryland, Virginia and New Jersey.

What is your favorite quote that can be printed on a T-Shirt, written on a mirror or wall?

One of my favorite quotes is from Michelle Obama. She said "Always stay true to yourself and never let what somebody else says, distract you from your goals." I remind myself of this quote often. There were a lot of people that told me that I would fail. As I would continue to say this quote on a daily basis, I started to believe in myself more and the things that people said no longer mattered.

What are the 6 major ingredients or components that have contributed to the formulation of your success as a young change maker thus far?

One of six major components that have contributed to my success has been just simply being a young entrepreneur. I think so many people see shows featuring kids with business ideas and develop

141

a belief that kid entrepreneurs are just made for reality TV. So, they're surprised when they actually have the opportunity to meet a young successful entrepreneur. My age has really helped a lot with the growth of my business. That's not to take away from all the hard work that I put into the operation of my business. But it sure doesn't hurt that my age has been a contributing factor. I have even had people just donate resources to help my business along.

Second, Vision. I always wanted to be my own boss. It started when I went to a seminar about girl empowerment about 4-plus years ago. I met a young entrepreneur Gabrielle Jordan, who was 13 years old at the time. While speaking with her, she told me to dream big and I have always kept those words close to my heart. When I first decided to start a business, I knew that it had to be something that was a part of my vision. I started by trying to make jewelry, an idea that I tried to emulate from someone else. I quickly found out jewelry making was not what I really wanted to do. I always had a love for baking and often was told that my desserts were delicious. Despite it all, I wanted to keep baking as a hobby and not so much as a business. As I continued to try different business idea, I realized that with each idea I tried there was no passion. The more and more family and friends complimented my desserts, the more I started to realize that starting a pastry business was my true calling. Miss Jordan told me, "when starting a business, it should be something that you are passionate about and have fun doing..." Baking was my passion and it was definitely fun for me.

Third, Support. I can't stress that enough. Having the support of family and friends has contributed greatly to my success. When I first shared my vision, there was immediate support. My support not only came physically and emotionally, but also financially. Running a business is literally an investment. When my family and friends, without hesitation, offered financial support, I knew that was one less thing I had to worry about. Had I not had an enormous amount of support, I don't know how far I would have been able to carry the business. One thing to remember is, support is not just having family and friends surrounding you, but also having mentors that are constantly providing you advice.

Fourth, have a Business Plan. At first, I just managed my business as orders came. I really didn't have a clear plan. I was just running a business. As the business grew, things started to become very confusing and I realize that I needed to really sit down and figure out what I wanted for my business. I wanted to be able to show that I was a legitimate business owner and could hold my own conversation just like any other business owner. A business plan basically was an outline for such conversation. A business plan helped me establish the direction of where I wanted to take my business and helped me stay on course on meeting specific goals. A business plan is also beneficial because when applying for certain certifications, it's a requirement.

Fifth, Mentors. Having mentors has been one of the greatest aspects of running my business. I have learned so much from them. I thought that it would be easy to run a business by myself. I would search Google for answers to questions that I had. There would be so much information that I didn't know what direction to go. As the aspects of operating a business began to become confusing, I finally decided to reach out to my mentors for guidance. Utilizing my mentors have been instrumental in my business' growth. I've learned so many business management aspects that I would have not known by just using Google or through trial and error. I also realized that having mentors in other areas of business can be helpful to your success. I've met a lot of amazing kid entrepreneurs thru social media and by joining various groups. I have found that obtaining advice from them or just being able to talk to them about the challenges helped a lot as well. It's great to have mentors because they will hold you accountable, so you can stay on course of achieving you dream.

Finally, Dedication. You have to show a high level of dedication if you want to see your vision come to life. When I first mentioned that I wanted to start a business, my mom told me that it would not be easy. That I really needed to understand that I would have to dedicate a lot of my time if I wanted the business to be a success. She explained that I would have to sacrifice a lot. She gave me a week to think about whether this was something that I truly wanted to do. Once I decided that I wanted to see my vision through, I knew that I had give a certain level of dedication to making my dream come true. I knew that being a young entrepreneur, I wouldn't be able to do a lot of things that other kids or my friends would do. I realized in order for me to make this business thing work, I had to be dedicate to my vision. It also meant that my family would have to show a level of dedication in helping me see my vision through. When someone asks about setting up a business, I always tell them to find a support group that will be just as dedicated as you are.

What does your typical business or work day look like? When do you fit in fun, school, friends and family?

During the school year, my typical day starts around 6 a.m. I usually check my email to see if any orders, speaking engagements or appearance requests have come in. I usually will set out an hour to read and respond to any inquiries. I will make sure to calendar any orders or events to make sure that there isn't any overbooking. I try to accomplish as much as I can during that hour, anything after that I give those duties over to my mom to finish. I try to stay on track of getting ready for school by 7 a.m. When school is over, the first thing I do is complete any homework assignments. School comes first. Once I complete my assignments, I'll go and check my email again for any new orders, inquiries or any follow up questions from prior emails. Also, if I have any upcoming events or orders, I'll contact the customer which is usually 72 hours before the delivery date to confirm all details of the order. It's also at this time full payment is required. In addition, I'll make sure to do an inventory check every Friday and make purchases to replenish my stock. When out of school for the summer, it's pretty much the same routine like being in school just minus the homework. I'm up by 8 a.m. and I'll usually experiment more with new recipes. Summertime usually brings a lot more catering events so I'm usually on the move a lot more. Although running a business is rewarding, my mom makes it a point that I still have time to enjoy my childhood. She makes it mandatory that at least one weekend out of the month that I spend time with friends. I think this helps a lot so I don't become overworked and stressed. In the beginning, I didn't like taking the time off because I wanted to be considered a legitimate business owner. Looking back, I think taking time off was a good idea. It gives me the time to relax and refocus on the direction of my business. To be honest, going to school full-time and running a business at the same time did become overwhelming. But once time was set out to enjoy time with friends it made managing school and the operations of my business a lot easier. Also Sundays are my days of rest. This time is spent in church and time with my family. Usually this is the time that we gather for dinner and/or enjoy each other's company.

What would you say success means to you? Why is it so important?

Success to me means believing in yourself and in your product. Taking a leap to start the business at a young age, you have already made a successful move. Some people, whether it's family, friends or anyone else, would equate success when you're making six or seven figures. I don't necessarily believe that to be true. While making six or seven figures is nice and an achievable dream for some, it should not be your only definition of success. Believing in yourself and your product is so important because only you know what you want. If you allow other people to tell you what and how your business should be, then it's no longer your business it's theirs. If you allow other people to define success by adding a dollar amount, then you will stress yourself out trying to reach someone's dream and definition of success. If you don't believe in yourself or your product, how can you expect anyone else to. If President Barack Obama didn't believe that he would become president, history would be different right now. If Oprah Winfrey didn't believe in herself, would she be one of the most influential woman in the world? If Steve Jobs didn't believe in himself, would we know Apple as we know it today? I would say just believe in yourself. Success doesn't define you. You define success.

How important would you say it is to be connected to other young people doing amazing things? How did you make these connections?

It is very important to connect with other young people. It was my connection with a young mogul that inspired me to start my business. I found that connecting with other young moguls will help you find or decide what your passion is, and then learn how to implement that passion into a business. I also believe that by connecting with other young moguls, you'll find the support and guidance that you need that's coming from somebody that's your age. I made the connection with other young moguls by searching social media, following or liking their pages and eventually reaching out to them. I don't limit my connection to just my industry. I've made sure to connect with young moguls from different industries because there's always something that can be learned to increase your level of success.

How important would you say reading and research is to the success of your business? What 3 business books would you recommended?

It was very important for me to read and research starting a business. Before I launch my business I did an extensive amount of research. I wanted to make sure that I understood the basic steps of starting a business before even launching. Not only did I want to understand the basic steps, I wanted to ensure that I understood the management aspects of a business. Books I recommend you should read are: ***The Making of a Young Entrepreneur: A Kids Guide to Developing the Mindset for Success*** by Gabrielle Jordan. Meeting Miss Jordan was actually the first time I had seen a kid entrepreneur. This was actually the first book that I read that spoke about how she became an entrepreneur and proactive plans to build the foundation of your business. Another book I read was, ***Better than a Lemonade Stand: Small Business Ideas for Kids*** by Daryl Bernstein. This book gives an outline of potential business ideas for young people to consider. It's the perfect book if you don't know what type of business you would like to start. Finally, ***Starting a Business for Dummies*** by Colin Barrow. While the title may include dummies, it really isn't saying you're a dummy. It's only implying that the context is easy for anyone to understand. This book gives you a step-by-step guideline of getting your business from just a dream to being fully operational.

If you could advise a future young mogul to do 3 things before starting their business what would that be?

I would say one, find what your passion is and turn that passion into your business idea. There's nothing better than doing something that you love and making money while doing it. Two, support. Make sure you have support from someone whether it be family or friends. And then, I would say find a mentor. You want someone that will be able to encourage you, give you honest advice and to just help you along the way. Having more than one mentor is fine as well. I have four mentors in different areas. I have a young mogul as a mentor, Gabrielle Jordan, who inspired me to start my business and continues to provide me advice, a mentor in the baking industry and financial and media industries mentors. It's very important to have someone, outside of family and friends, that can go along with you through your journey.

What are 3 lessons you have learned so far as a CEO, Founder or Public Figure?

Three lessons that I have learned are: Time management. In the beginning, I thought I had everything under control. I was so used to being able to manage small orders with no problem and no real planning except to have the order ready by the due date. As the customers started to increase and the volume of orders started to increase, I could no longer continue with that carefree mentality. It took one incident (which was one too many) of not keeping track of time and I didn't deliver an order at the time requested. While the customer was

146

very understanding, not all customers will be that way. I learned quickly that I had to manage my time more effectively and adjust it to reflect the growth of my operation. Another aspect is networking. I can't express how important networking is. I found that in order for my business to reach this level of success, I had to get out there and talk to people. I learned a valuable lesson of networking when my mom attended a seminar and talked about my business to the attendees. Although she wasn't able to stay long, it was a brief conversation about my business that lead to the creation of a conference in my county for future young entrepreneurs. It has also led to media appearances, speaking engagements and interviews. I not only learned that networking opens the door for various opportunities, it provides free advertisement. Your ability to speak to a crowd of people at no cost and ultimately have these same people go back to their communities, jobs, etc and talk about your business with only help your business' growth. Finally, I learned that marketing is important because no one will know about your business if you don't put it out there. I learned that in order to reach a large group of people, I had to utilize other marketing techniques besides word-of-mouth from family and friends only. The biggest marketing tool that I've recently started using a lot of is social media. Social media has become a very important marketing tool to advertise my business. I have also utilized promotional products and promoted specials to garner potential customers.

Where do you pull inspiration from?

I pull my inspiration from my mom. Watching her fulfill her obligation to the military and then coming home giving her all to support and care for me is too hard to put into words. Just watching how she commanded respect and at the same time managed an entire department with ease, was so amazing. She would constantly have conversations with me about working hard to get what you want, but to never compromise yourself in your pursuit. Watching her operate in her gift of leadership, I knew that I wanted to be exactly like her. I knew that if I wanted something a certain way, then don't compromise my expectation for how I wanted it to be. Being able to see her work in the capacity that she did inspired me to manage my business in the same manner. Also, seeing her love for God reminds me that this is not all my doing but by divine revelation and guidance.

What are 3 specific challenges you have had as a young mogul? How have you been able to overcome them?

Three challenges that I have come across as a young mogul are not being able to hang with friends or attend school events. Owning a business takes a lot of sacrifice. Sometimes you're just not able to do the things that your friends or your peers are able to do. While sometimes I'm disappointed that I can't do all the things that my friends do, I remind myself that I have a bigger vision and to reach my goal I can't do or go to everything. Despite the sacrifices, I do make it a point to schedule at least one day a month to relax, to spend time with my friends. I always tell myself that while I maybe missing out on something that may result in temporary resentment, my vision is something that will have a lasting impact on my life. Another challenge is, running a business will sometimes require long days and nights. During the school year, I have to make it a point to balance out the time of doing school work then going over the aspects of the business. Depending on how much schoolwork I may have will determine how much time I'll have to spend on the business. There have been times when I only had about four hours of sleep as I prepare for large events. Usually during times when I don't get much sleep, I'll take the next day to fully relax and recover. As my business continues to grow, I'm looking at employing family and/or friends to help with larger events. I think by hiring employees it will alleviate some of the long days and nights. Also another challenge, in the beginning, was having people just not recognizing me as a business owner. They would see me with my mom and would automatically assume that she was the business owner. When I would tell them I'm the owner, there would always be a look of surprise and doubt. So, I would spend a lot of time explaining that I'm the owner and she is actually my employee. With a customer base of very prominent corporations and influential individuals, I believe those that doubted have now recognized me as a legitimate business owner.

What are your goals for the future? What's next?

My future goals are to become a celebrity pastry chef, open pastry shops in New York and Los Angeles, and have my pastries sold in grocery stores across the nation. I would also like to go to Paris and study how to make authentic French pastries. Next for me is that I would like to write a children's book on overcoming the stresses of being bullied and converting that negativity into positive self-worth. I would also like to continue sharing my story through various speaking engagements not just on overcoming bullying but on how to become a young successful entrepreneur.

I am the Founder/CEO of Glorious Pastries by Gabrielle and I started my business at 9 years old.

My mission is to help youth find their passion and turn it into a successful business. In my business, I help young people and parents to understand how to remove negative societal pressures and move to a more positive way of thinking. I am also a Pageant Queen, a First-Degree Black Belt, College Student (at 14 years old), and a Motivational Speaker. I hope to be able to work with you and help you understand that you can be the next Warren Buffet or Steve Jobs by just believing in yourself and in your dream(s).

ACKNOWLEDGEMENTS

A very special thank you to those who have supported my journey and helped me turn my dreams into a reality...

Vernice Williams (Mommy); Emery, Shirah, Aubrey and Makenzie Simmons; Michelle Pope; Ronte Murphy; Kim, Romanda, Cameron and Kendall Thompson; Gregory Pope; Jerry & Yvonne Celestine; Jonathan Powell; Pamela Pratt; Summaiyya Lee; Chief Designz; DFitness Teresa Alvarez; Lisa Holmes; Luciette Wren; Wesley Hopkins; Marcy Patrick; Tracey Whiteman; Bryan D.; Sr. and Rochelle Jones

Chapter XX. Generation Impact: Be a Force for Good
Temi and Tami Oniyitan

www.mimis.com.ng
Facebook.com/mimisexplorers
Instagram.com/mimisexplorers
Twitter.com/MimisExplorers

Temi and Tami Oniyitan are enterprising twin sisters, Founders and CEOs of the "Mimi's" brand. They founded Mimi's in 2017 when they were 7 years old, with the launch of Mimi's Mocktails & Juices at the KENT Fair. Since then, they have launched Mimi's Academy, Mimi's Adventure Book Series and Mimi's Essentials.

Their passion to create multiple businesses is fueled by their passion to make a difference and inspire others, especially children. Temi and Tami contribute their profits and donations from their campaigns to their Mimi's Give Back Initiative, from which they pay school fees, provide school supplies, organize book drives, etc. for children from low-income families in Nigeria. They have also volunteered at Unveiling Africa Foundation's Christmas Soup Kitchen to feed 700 underprivileged children, and Beautiful Onyinye Foundation's Easter Outreach to Royal Diamond Orphanage.

They have shared stories about their businesses and humanitarian work with children and adults at various events such as the Childpreneur Boot Camp, Goal Setting and Vision Board Boot Camp and Kobby Kids Club, among others.

Temi and Tami have been featured on various local and international media platforms including CultureTree, Kids of the Kosmos and Juniority TV. They are recipients of the Best Appearance prize at the KENT Fair in 2017, Humanitarian of the Year award from the prestigious Nigerian Child Summit and Awards, Kidpreneur Ambassador award from Kidpreneur Africa and the SDG Badge (for their work on the United Nations Sustainable Development Goal 4: Quality Education) from the Nigerian Child Initiative, all in 2018. They are also ambassadors for Future4Kids Africa and the International Daddy-Daughter Day Out.

The twins express themselves in various ways like karate, swimming, music, dance, drama and track. They love to learn, read and travel around the world (through their imagination, on Google and in real life).

What is your favorite quote that can be printed on a T-shirt, written on a mirror or wall?

Our favorite quote is so simple. Here it goes. "Doing good is good business." It's just five simple words, but yet so deep, and we would absolutely love to have these words printed on a T-shirt or written on a mirror or wall to inspire others.

It all boils down to being good. Being good to those who work with you, good to those who buy from you, good to your neighbors, good to your environment, good to your community, good to your nation. Just be good, and you will never regret it.

As we help children from poor families from the money from our businesses, doing good is the number one key to our success. The world will be so much better if we are all good to one another. We should all treat others in the way that is best good for them. This is our Secret Sauce.

Our mom told us that this is one of the greatest legacies her mum (our grandmother), Antonia Obafunke Motolani taught her before she passed on. Her goodness continues to live on in the great stories people tell about her many years after she has gone. This is the same with Nelson Mandela, Wangari (Mother of Trees), Dr. Martin Luther King Jr. and Mother Teresa, among many others.

What are the 6 major ingredients or components that have contributed to the formulation of your success as a young change-maker thus far?

We're going to give you six major ingredients that have contributed to the formulation of our success as a young change-maker.

First ingredient discover your PURPOSE. Everyone was put on earth for a purpose, and we all need to discover it. It may not be easy to discover your purpose early, but if you continue to explore like we did, you will eventually discover it. Our mom first helped us in discovering our purpose by asking us the question, "What change do you want to see in the world?" We've also used vision boards and goal-setting exercises to help the discovery process. The more you explore, the more you get clear on things which will eventually lead you to your purpose.

Second is PASSION. You need to do things that give you joy and make you happy. If you're not happy with what you do, you will not be successful doing it. Sometimes your passion may shift or change, but the end goal is for you to find what really makes you happy deep within your heart. Let your passion always drive you.

Third is DETERMINATION. You must find your inner strength, have faith and believe that you can change the world no matter your age, race, background or any other factor. If you are truly determined, you'll find a way around challenges that come up. You need to always try. Our mom always tells us that if you shoot for the moon and you miss, you will still land on the stars. The secret is to always try and put in your very best.

Forth is CONFIDENCE. You need to have confidence in yourself and what you can do. If you are not 100% sure that you can achieve your dreams, you will keep finding excuses. Never doubt yourself and even if those thoughts come up, tell yourself you can do it. You have all you need to succeed within you. Look in the mirror every day and tell yourself: I am the one the world has been waiting for. I am a changemaker.

Fifth is accepting that "No" IS NOT A BAD RESPONSE. Not everyone will like what you do. Even if you are raising money for the poor like we do, someone will still not believe in what you're doing and they will still say "No" to you. Hearing the word "No" can be hard, but don't let it affect you. "NO" simply means Next Opportunity. Just move on.

152

Sixth ingredient is DO IT. Just get it done. Stop talking and start doing. Don't overthink it. Our mom tells us that if you look at the first version of your work and you are not embarrassed, then you did too much thinking. So just start what you think you want to do, get feedback and then get better from there. Take small steps but keep moving forward in the right direction.

Mixing all of these six ingredients with "doing good," which is our ultimate Secret Sauce, is what has made us who we are thus far.

What does your typical business or work day look like? When do you fit in fun, school, friends and family?

Our typical work days right now are evenings during school days, weekends and holidays. Since we have multiple businesses, our typical work day depends on what product or service we are providing. Let us use our mocktail business as an example. Work starts before the actual day because we need to buy items we will use from the fruit market and the store. If we are serving the mocktails fresh in cups, we visit the ice factory first to buy ice and we make the mocktails at the venue of the fair, party or event. We set up at the location and serve our customers there. We recently started bottling our mocktails to serve at venues, or for delivery directly to our customers. For that, we produce a night before so that we can get it frozen to preserve it.

On days we sell or serve, we decide the roles each one of us will be playing: Getting customers, serving mocktails, taking cash and giving change, talking about our humanitarian work, getting feedback on the quality of our work, cleaning up and so on. At the end of the day, we calculate all that we have made and apply the "3 S" formula our mom taught us -- how much of the money are we going to SAVE (in the bank and our education fund), SEED (as tithe and for our humanitarian work) and SPEND (to buy things the business needs and we need). For pre-booked events where customers pay directly into our bank account, we still apply the same formula.

Business is fun for us. We get to meet new people, learn new things and interact with children and adults, but we definitely still schedule time for fun. School has its own scheduled timing and we respect that. As part of the balancing act, we invite our friends and family to join us while we work. It is, however, a priority in our home to have private family activities and play dates with our friends. We also

153

schedule time for our humanitarian work, when we visit the children we support as they become our friends in the process.

What would you say success means to you? Why is it so important?

Success means a lot of different things to different people. The true meaning of success for us is the difference we are able to make in the lives of others no matter what we do. Success for us is waking up every morning and going through the day feeling happy and putting a smile on everybody's face we interact with, ensuring that we are spreading happiness. That is why our business tagline "a burst of happiness" links directly to our definition of success.

This is very important to us because in our world today, there is so much unhappiness everywhere. We believe that if we are able to make people happy, we're as good as saving a life and making the world a better place. And what better way to measure your success.

How important would you say it is to be connected to other young people doing amazing things? How did you make these connections?

It is very important to us that we connect to other young people doing amazing things. You see, not everyone agrees with the way we are being brought up by our parents. A lot of people think it's too much, say we are too young and that right now we should just focus on going to school and making good grades. For us to keep our motivation up, we need to surround ourselves with like-minded young people doing awesome stuff. Our mom and dad say, "Show me your friends and I'll tell you who you are." If our friends are doing amazing things, then we sure will do amazing things, too.

We make a lot of connections in the course of doing our business. Our line of businesses involve a lot of face-to-face interactions and networking. In addition, we attend conferences, boot camps and other events for children that help us meet new people. We also get to meet people via social media, though our mom manages our pages. She lets us see the new connections we make on a regular basis and allows us respond to messages under her supervision. Instagram and Facebook have been major for us, but we also use Twitter.

How important would you say reading and research is to the success of your business? What 3 business books would you recommend?

154

Reading & Research are very important for us in all that we do. We are avid readers. We have a budget for books every term. We read a lot of books because it helps us explore in our minds. Research for us is beyond reading. It also involves a lot of interactions with people, attending trainings, exhibitions and expos, asking questions, observing people and things. All these have been critical to our success. We learn from reading and research as it helps to learn from others which has proven to be very useful.

Our top three favorite business books for now are:

#3 *The Young Entrepreneur's Guide to Starting and Running a Business* by Steve Mariotti. Like the name states, it serves as a guide, providing step-by-step guidance for starting and running a business. Our mom had this book in the house as far back as we can remember. She has always used this book as reference for teaching us.

#2 *Kidpreneurs* by Matthew and Adam Toren. Our mom bought us this book to provide us with a simpler and age-appropriate way of learning about business and entrepreneurship.

#1 *Minipreneur* is written by our mom, Olanrewaju Oniyitan and it holds a special place in our hearts. When we were 5 years old, she searched for an age-appropriate book on teaching kids about business and entrepreneurship. The few she got were international books that had snow packing, dog walking and babysitting as examples. At that time, we could not really relate with these examples since we lived in Nigeria (West Africa), and so she decided not to sit and complain, she provided a solution and wrote a book herself with us as part of the major characters. Today, we are 8+ years and have launched our various businesses based on principles from the book. This book is currently being translated to French as well.

If you could advise a future young mogul to do 3 things before starting their business what would they be?

Dear Future Young Mogul,

You are here because you want to start your business and don't know where to begin. From our experience, these are the three things you should definitely do before taking the leap.

One, identify your passion and link it to your business. It just makes it easier. Our business started out of our passion to raise money to help poor children to go to school. It is the same passion that has led us to the creation of our other businesses.

Two, have a plan. It doesn't have to be a complex one. Our mom helped us with a one-page plan from her *Minipreneur* book for our first business. It gave us some clarity on what to do. Is it the same plan we have now? No. It has definitely changed based on customer feedback, but the initial plan helped us get started.

Three, have a support system. You need to have the right people around you to support you. These support pillars will help you hold your business dreams in place. Trust us. You need it. You need mentors, champions, connectors, and even critics to help you in your business.

With these three things, you are on a great path to starting your business. Good luck!

Yours in business,

Temi and Tami Oniyitan

What are 3 lessons you have learned so far as a CEO, founder or public figure?

The three lessons we have learned as CEOs, founders and public figures are....

Number One, there is no shortcut to success. You have to pay your dues. If you think you are young and people will just support you, you are wrong. Every customer wants value for their money, even if it is a donation to a charitable cause. So, you need to do what you do very well. Success only happens when opportunity meets preparation. You need to do your work. Play your part. Even if it means nothing now. One day, the opportunity will come for you to showcase what you have done. So, start doing the work now.

Number Two, failing is not a bad thing. In our part of the world, failing is like a taboo. But failing at something doesn't mean you are a failure, as long as you have learned from your mistakes and move forward. Failure is actually a good teacher. Good decisions come from having experience. But experience come from bad decisions. That's just life. Like our mom says, learn from your mistakes and move on.

Number Three, you must always reinvent yourself. You cannot remain stagnant. You need to add value to your business and grow.

Once you achieve success, you should already be considering how you will transform the business to its next stage. Always test and explore ways to reinvent yourself and your business to stay relevant.

Where do you pull inspiration from?

We pull inspiration first from God, who put us on this earth for a purpose. We also draw inspiration from our mom because she helps us all the time in everything that we do. Our mom went the whole nine yards to write a book for us on entrepreneurship called *Minipreneur* because she could not find a local resource for us. Our dad also inspires us a lot. He ditches the African and Nigerian Father stereotype and does everything within his reach to support our dreams.

We also pull inspiration from places and things when we travel the world in our imagination, on Google and in real life. We are always looking for inspiration for our business and even school work.

We get even more inspiration from the stories of our late grandmother that our mom tells us. She was a phenomenal businesswoman and a huge giver. She was known for giving to a lot of people who still talk about her many years after her passing. We are also inspired by other world-changers like Nelson Mandela, Wangari (Mother of Trees), Dr. Martin Luther King Jr. and Mother Teresa Their lives have taught us that, "Leaders are givers."

What are 3 specific challenges you have had as a young mogul? How have you been able to overcome them?

We have come to accept that we will always face challenges as young moguls.

Our first challenge is getting to agree on what is best for the business, since it's run by two of us. Even though we're twins, we like different things. We come up with different ideas all the time. So, what do we do to overcome this challenge? We get an independent person to look at what is in the best interest for our business. For now, that neutral party is our mom and dad.

Our second challenge is managing what we do with school. It has been really tough for us to manage multiple businesses and humanitarian work with school work. But we have learned a lot about time management: how we can schedule activities and plan our time.

Our mom also does a great job of linking our school work with our business so now we are even more enthusiastic about school.

Our third and final challenge is balancing our passion for giving to the poor with ensuring that our business is profitable. Left to us, we would give all the money we make to poor children. Our mom has helped in overcoming this by teaching us about financial literacy and taking us on trainings on how to manage our money. That way we have been able to better balance our humanitarian work with our business.

What are your goals for the future? What's next?

We envision a world where every child has access to education. Education is every child's right. And we will do all that we can to make it happen, especially for children from poor families. This vision continues to drive us. We will also go a step further to teach others to see what we see so that they can change the world with us. There is an African proverb that says "It takes a village to raise a child." Well, we are part of that village and we will do all that we can to ensure poor children have access to education, even though we are children ourselves.

While we are doing that, we will continue to build great business empires that will help us achieve our goals so that even when people decide not to give, our profits are large enough to fund our humanitarian work. In doing all of this, we will continue pursue our own education to the highest level, in line with our dreams. We believe in the power of education.

We look forward to the day we can pay school fees for 1,000 children and provide our HOPE School Bags filled with back-to-school items to 10,000 children. Our dream is to someday own a school where we provide free education, food and healthcare for children from low-income families.

We are Temi and Tami Oniyitan, twin Founders and CEOs of the Mimi's brand made up of Mimi's Mocktails & Juices, Mimi's Academy, Mimi's Adventure Book Series, Mimi's Essentials and Mimi's Give Back Initiative. We started our journey with our first business when we were 7 years old. Our mission is to motivate, inspire and encourage children and youths around the world to do what they love, dream BIG, make their dreams come true and use their success to make the world a better place. In our business, we help children, youths and adults experience a burst of happiness through our mocktails, juices, books, speaking engagements,

trainings, essential items and humanitarian work focused on education for the poor. We are ambassadors for entrepreneurship and social good. We also love reading, writing, travelling, karate, swimming, music, dance, drama and track. We hope to be able to work with you, and help you learn to become a leader, entrepreneur and change-maker.

ACKNOWLEDGEMENTS

A very special thank you to those who have supported our journey and helped us turn our dreams into a reality...

Obafunke Antonia Olaofe; Oluwaseyifunmi Leona Ogundele; Ademide Okubena; Adebimpe & Adebukunmi Adebogun; Daniella & Samantha Soje; Moyinoluwa & Morounfoluwa Oluwaseun; Ebunoluwa Olaopa; Seun & Tise Oniyitan; Ireoluwa Sawyerr; Vincent & Juliet Obi; Juliet Alozie; Omon Obike; Oluwaseun Ogundele; Adesola Adeuga; Anuoluwapo Oderinde; Uche John; Basira Olateju Ojora-Adejiyan; Abraham Oshoko;Timi Onabolu; Tope Aremo

Chapter XXI. The Science Behind Basketball is a Slam Dunk to My Growth, and Success!

Shamar James Anderson

www.shajanderenterprise.com
Facebook.com/ShaJanderEnterprise
Instagram.com/shamarjamesanderson
Twitter.com/ShaJanderEnterp

Shamar James Anderson is a young authorpreneur and entrepreneur who is very loving and very compassionate. Shamar is working to be a game-changer, and is focused on excelling in academics, basketball and entrepreneurship.

He was born and raised in Georgia, United States of America. Shamar prides himself on promoting the power of passion and perseverance to accomplish nothing but greatness. This came about due to overcoming adversity at a very early age. His love for basketball drives him to practice daily in order to become his best. He experienced that in order to be successful, it is important to like what you do, and this will be the driving force centered around everything else. He strives to empower others to be successful in every facet of their lives, despite any challenges. He also encourages parents to support their children's dreams and be their advocate.

A lifelong basketball player, Shamar is intrigued that science plays an important role in the game. His love of basketball began at an early age and now he spends his years under the guidance of a former professional basketball player who fostered his love of the sport and helps to perfect his skill set.

In his first book, Shamar will use the science of basketball to encourage kids to develop their skills because lessons learned in sports are transferable to the individual as a whole and other parts of life. His goal is to encourage kids to be brave, confident, strong and determined; and they can be successful at any age.

He and his father recorded an original song, "Stop the Hate", which will soon be released worldwide.

Shamar is a second-degree World Taekwondo Federation black belt, enjoys playing video games, and spending time with his friends and family. He loves to travel and often visits and explores different states in the U.S., and cities in other countries.
The science of basketball fuels his drive to excel in his academics, attitude, business and everything else. He played several sports before and committed to Taekwondo for many years. Despite the fact that martial arts taught him discipline and to believe in himself, basketball was different. It was the sport that changed his balance forever, and one that is molding him to become successful in all areas.

Shamar's mind is set on pursuing his studies at Duke University, making it on their basketball team, and upon graduation, playing for the the National Basketball Association (NBA). With that said, he knows good attitude, footwork and excellence are some of the ingredients needed to accomplish those goals. He is fierce in making it happen. Despite his challenges in school at an early age, with the great support system from mom, school and educators, Shamar is determined to overcome adversity.

Shamar owns his own T-shirt company, Shajander Wears Inc., and is working on designing and adding belts to the product list.

In addition, Shamar is also a photographer and videographer for I Hear You Inc., a non-profit organization whose mission is to give the gift of hearing to kids who are d/Deaf and hard of hearing in the Caribbean. This is a project inspired by a real-life experience, with support of his mother.

Shamar's goal is to encourage kids to be confident, focused, and that success can be formulated at any age.

One of Shamar's favorite quotes, "I think it goes hand in hand because if you discipline yourself on the floor, as you become an older player or a more seasoned individual, it adds structure in your life." Dominique Wilkins

What does your typical business or work day look like? When do you fit in fun, school, friends and family?

Thus far, my mom works with me in managing my business and teaching me the fundamentals. However, we do have some routines that we follow everyday as it is important for me and my chief operating officer (COO), who is my mom, to be on the same page. Day to day we do the following:

1. Monitor and engage on social media.
2. Monitor sales from Shajander Enterprise (book), and Shajander Wears Inc.
4. Discuss vendors, quality of T-shirt samples, progress, budget, competitors, opportunity for improvement, targeting markets and buyers, investing, banking, community service, vending opportunities and future projects.
5. Follow other young moguls/entrepreneurs, watch their interviews and study their best practices to be successful.
6. Network, and attend other vending opportunities.

I attend transitional school so it is important to balance my time for homework, studies, basketball training and other activities. We also focus on not being distracted so we remain focused on driving business growth, and gauge in the future expansion.

I fit in fun every day as I play basketball, which is the driving force in everything I do. During the school year, I play basketball before going to school and between homework and other activities after school. During the week or weekends, my neighborhood friends join me in playing basketball. During the weekend and summer months, I enjoy playing with other friends through planned activities or through video games online.

Mostly during school breaks and summer, I hang with my friends through camp, going to the gym to play basketball or in my neighborhood as well or going to a basketball game or to an amusement park.

What is your favorite quote that can be printed on a T-shirt, written on a mirror or wall?

Passion and Perseverance are the key to Success!

Through the passion for basketball and my endless drive to train to become the best, I encounter that in order to be successful, it is important to like what you do while being persistent. It is called grit -- the power of passion and perseverance. Life now becomes a marathon to set and achieve goals by working hard at it every day. Basketball keeps me motivated, developing and getting better all-around in life. It is teaching me values on how to exceed all around, and I am using that in this everyday life. The science of basketball is teaching me balance, to remain focused, to believe in myself, and reach for the sky in using the same concepts with the science behind success.

Blossoming and performing well are all part of success. Community involvement and making a difference is also the core in a successful business. The passion to play ball and to strive to make it to the NBA are part of my goals. Therefore my effort is pretty much valuable to the goal I want to achieve. It is important for me to discipline myself to win.

The 6 major components that have contributed to the formulation of my success as a young change-maker thus far are as follows:

1. The passion I have for playing basketball while striving to become one of the best basketball players, so I can be a National Basketball Association (NBA) candidate transforms me to be the best in everything I do.
2. Faith through the power of prayer, and constant delivery of prayers for me by my mom
3. Confidence to overcome adversity and believe in myself
7. Fortunate to have a phenomenal mom, family and educators who care about me and are always motivating me and supporting me.
8. Transforming the passion for fine art and using it to start my business in designing T-shirt products.
9. Being an avid traveler, which allows me to explore and value other people and their cultures. In addition, I am able to appreciate the opportunity to travel.

The above-mentioned ingredients came about in my life within the past three years. It is about the same time I became serious about playing basketball and I wanted to dedicate my time to that sport and not any other. I found my connection there. I did not mind spending countless time on the court or in my front yard. I then realize that I had to maintain good grades and began to put that same effort into my academics. The science behind the bouncing ball is my driving force. I use force to push the ball toward the basket, friction to move it along the court and gravity to jump to get a shot in the basket. However, before getting on the court I have to make sure that my ball is filled with air which are tiny molecules to make bounciness on the court possible. I have to be physically fit by making sure I have a balance of nutrients in my body. I have to exercise so I can perform well. I use this same concept in my daily life in order to accomplish success. The science behind basketball gives me the power to be my best all around. In order to achieve my goals, I have to be well-rounded. I have to be disciplined in being motivated to achieve. This part is the anatomy of how I program myself to win. Winning is the science called mastery. It was only then my attitude changed, and I began applying the same principle to do great in academics. Even though I dislike one subject, the mindset is that all the subjects are part of the ingredients to succeed so I have to be persistent and give my best in order for all of me to be successful. It takes the same to run and operate a business. I cannot be successful in business if I do not have the passion for what I am doing. The passion to design T-shirts came about as my love for fine art and being fascinated with Gucci brand. For the past couple years, I asked my mom for a Gucci T-shirt or belt for Christmas or my birthday, and she said to me, "No, design and wear your own, you can do it." It is my hobby, and I design shirts on my Xbox for myself as a character in NBA 2K18 game. That is where my aspiration to design and sell T-shirts began. However, my mom explained to me that we cannot sell the T-shirts I designed on that platform since they are licensed merchandise. From this conversation, my aspiration developed and I started with the Wakanda and basketball idea. I also designed my first sneaker on nike.com with my name on it. It came out well as my dad purchased it for me for Christmas 2017. I was amazed at the final product and wanted to turn it into a money-making venture. Eventually, I still hope to purchase Gucci brand. I believe that businesses should support each other.

What would you say success means to you? Why is it so important?

Success can be different for everyone. However, for me, it is a skill to show up positive in all areas of one's life living a life that makes me feel proud of myself while following God's will as being obedient. It means living life in abundance where everything is positive. Good health and accomplishments all around. Striving to have excellent grades to attend one of the best universities, eating healthy, keeping fit, aspiring to be a National Basketball Association player and maintaining healthy relationships with everyone.

Giving back to the community is a big piece of this pie as well. Success is important because it gives one peace of mind, and it is something designed and measured by oneself. It is the daily efforts that drive our goals to become a reality to be successful. I will continue to set goals and measure my progress of continuous growth, development and constant improvement. Others are watching, and as I empower other children, it is important to continue my drive and leave footprints, and eventually a legacy. Success will allow me to grow in confidence, inspire others, become an interesting icon and able to achieve any goal I wants through confidence, and the power to block anything negative.

How important would you say it is to be connected to other young people doing amazing things? How did you make these connections?

It is important to be connected to other young people doing amazing things because since their aspiration is the same, they will support you and elevate you to continue winning. They are role models and an inspiration to watch grow. Actually, I am currently experiencing this with my personal social media and *The Science Behind It* book's social media pages. Parents of other young authors, entrepreneurs and children continue to be my biggest fans day to day. They are continuously encouraging and saying how proud they are. They are also very responsive to questions, suggestions or comments. They are game-changers. They are my biggest fans. Many have years of experience in the market and business-specific fields, so they can share their experience and guidance as well.

I am making these connections through social media pages, attending events and vending opportunities where many of my peers in this arena are in attendance. I tend not to be shy since it feels like family.

How important would you say reading and research is to the success of your business? What 3 business books would you recommend?

Reading and research are very important part of any business. My mom and I did a lot of research prior to selecting our print on demand drop shipping vendor including customer service ratings, quality and reliability reviews. We are also a member of a few online platforms that discuss branding and launching, and we took away a lot of information there from others in the same business as I am. My mom is also a member of Raising A Mogul Society, and she shared several information from there as well. The T-shirt industry is very competitive, but my goal is to empower youths and motivate others with expressions or quotes on the products. Marketing and target audience are also critical elements to research. Reading books from business owners and researching their progress are also important as many share their experience and share valuable information pertaining to pros and cons or their successes and failures. Their failures are a red flag shared for others to analyze.

The 3 books I would recommend are as follows:

1. *You Can Get It If You Really Want* by Levi Roots - This book was an easy read and very inspiring. Found great rules for business success together with several business tools, resources and advice. I love this book a lot since Levi Roots' passion for good cooking sauce is great for success. His brand is powerful, and his natural instinct and love for tasty food did it. When there is passion and perseverance, success is chemical reaction. Levi also encourages starters to go after their dream.
2. *How Did You Do It, Truett? A Recipe for Success* by Truett Cathy, founder and CEO of Chick-fil-A - This book offers lots about wisdom. As a business owner, this book shares about faith, principles/work ethic and the importance of family and community service. In order to be successful, one should give back, and it is an important ingredient. An awesome book that was easy to read and great for young people like myself or any starter in business.
3. *Smart Money Smart Kids: Raising the next Generation to Win with Money* by Dave Ramsey - Great information about the basics of money, saving and investment. I frequent the Federal Reserve Bank websites to download simple books on money. One cool one is *Great minds Think - A New Guide To Money* by the Federal Reserve Bank of Cleveland.

If you could advise a future young mogul to do 3 things before starting their business what would they be?

166

1. Make sure they are passionate in the business they are attempting to start and go for it!
2. Research about the market, competitors and the target audience.
4. Focus on how to be different from their competitors, and how to deliver nothing but greatness.

What are 3 lessons you have learned so far as a CEO, founder or public figure?

1. It is hard work but once you are passionate about something, the hard work becomes natural, and the goals become easier to accomplish because the passion of playing ball and the science behind it motivates me to focus on the ingredients needing to get there. For example, I know I have to make extremely good grades to get into the university of my choice, so despite the challenge I may have in math, I am forced to overcome the fear and do my best and establish a study plan to get better grades and eventually only A's. This same concept is the science of success in my business. I am motivated to be successful
2. It is a competitive market and you have to be creative to be different by adding extra values. I tend to target the young consumers and their parents.
3. There are many children like myself in the business world, and it is rewarding. I can still be a kid, enjoy pre-teen life and run a business. It just takes planning and managing time.

Where do you pull inspiration from?

I pull inspiration from my mom. She is phenomenal. She believes in me and is always by my side. She also continues to show me the way so I can become independent as a whole person and a successful business person. She continues to instill in me that education is important and that I should believe in myself and be capable of being the best. No one can define me. My mom continues to give me the tools needed to remain focus on my journey. I also want to give credit to my former principal and two of my former educators. They are Dr. Donna Bishop, Mrs. Bridgett Brown, and Mrs. Dawn Cooper. I am forever grateful for their contributions and making a difference in my life. I get my inspiration from them as well. Mrs. Brown instilled in me that I can do anything I put my mind to, and spent a time showing me reinforcement. It was only then I pulled myself together and believed in myself especially in math, a subject I felt that I couldn't do. It is my weakest subject and I was afraid of doing it, but now I am no longer afraid and give it my best. Mrs. Cooper from Kindergarten believed that I was capable of improving as I got older. Dr. Bishop was always supportive throughout and never gave up hope. She was also a part of change and continues to provide an awesome school community. I also want to give credit to Primrose School for my foundation before attending elementary school. I am forever thankful for a great support system.

What are 3 specific challenges you have had as a young mogul? How have you been able to overcome them?

The three challenges I had as a young mogul are as follows:

1. Balancing school, business and basketball
2. Not being a professional graphic artist
3. Not being able to spend money as I get it.

I overcame the first challenge by working around basketball training and practice to align with school and business. It was important to draft up a calendar with school, and basketball then we will plug in business meetings and activities. I overcame the challenges by learning more about SWOT. SWOT is a tool or technique used to evaluate ones strengths, weaknesses, opportunities and threats. My mom educated me on that and we checked on what my strengths was and worked around my weaknesses. I will draw my ideas and my mom will pay for a professional graphic designer to design my T-shirts so it is print ready. One of my cousins, Deirdre in London, recently this past summer organized a tour to the University of Art with a student there, Nan, who is a student from China. Nan gave me some valuable ideas, style, applications I can use or how to draw and iron onto T-shirts. There are so many processes and applications. I also attended an art exhibition where I saw displays from other students and was able to ask questions. She also introduced me to some software programs. And it is such a learning process! Thanks to my cousin for such a valuable connection.

I had to learn more about money management, what we invest in the business and how we have to make the money back before making a profit. I also learn that savings and investment are important. I took a class with Christon "The Truth" Jones on how to open a brokerage account and select stock, so I know more about how to invest.

What are your goals for the future? What's next?
I have a few things in the making to include working on my belt product

line for my business. I am fascinated with Gucci belts which I cannot afford currently but inspired and thrilled to work on my own line. I also have a song called "Stop The Hate", which I did with my dad in 2017. I am working on copyrights and getting it professionally recorded.

My goals for the future are to successfully finish school with excellent grades to attend Duke University and play for their basketball team. I love them for their career programs and basketball. My interest is to become a digital forensics expert and forensic computer investigator, and my desire is to get into the National Basketball Association (NBA). In the line of my business, to expand my business empire to the point where I can sell my product line wholesale to major department stores globally, while slowly removing the resale component.

Since I help my mom in photography and videography in her non-profit business, I would like to speak to her audience from time to time, empowering them to become their own boss and to believe in themselves. I want them to know that they have so much to give to this world and encourage them that they can. The thought of being an international speaker to targeted audiences such as youths in underserved communities. I just want to make a difference in others who are facing challenges. Currently, I participate in volunteering at food banks, and I want to eventually impact the life of other children by doing something great. I am planning to reach out to the schools to see what is needed the most in my community so I, too, can start a non-profit foundation to be part of the solution.

I am an author and the CEO of Shajander Enterprise, and Shajanda Wears Inc. I started my business at the age of 11 years old. I overcame adversity, and I have grit, a passion for basketball and perseverance to succeed. You can, too. I want to be a game-changer, I want to reach as many children as I can to inspire and empower them. I want them to know that they, too, can be successful despite any challenges. My mission is to empower and inspire young people. In my business. I help to fight hunger by volunteering at several Food Banks. I also deliver care packages with creative cards to Food Banks. I do believe that a card with encouraging words can make a difference in a child's life. My message to other children - The power of passion and perseverance are the key to success so go for it and turn your passion into making money today! You can also use what you are passionate about to make a difference in helping other children. Whether you love sports, visual or performing art, cooking or baking, or even science; take pride in developing it. Eventually, your passion can be the ticket to your success at any age.

ACKNOWLEDGEMENTS

A very special thank you to those who have supported my journey and helped me turn my dreams into a reality...

Cecilia Yvonne James; Michael T. Anderson; Shakiera Williams; Deirdre Pascall; Richard Nicholson; Jerry & Pat Nicholson; Joann Rose-Walker; Joscelyn Sylvester; Jefferson Glasgow; Coach Norris "Bo" Bell; Bridgett Brown; Joseph Forrester; Alex & Joyce Pascall; Dr. Jacob Nathaniel Thomas, M.D; Dr. Donna R. Bishop; Dawn Cooper; Lajuanda Hall; Uche, Najja & Nile Nicholson; Tanisha Turner; Phyllis Scipio & Earline Sylvester

Chapter XXII. Delphine's Formula to Success is Not Rocket Science
Delphine Nephtalie Dauphin

www.princessdelphine.com
Facebook.com/joysyummycupcakesbydel
Instagram.com/cupcakesbydel
Twitter.com/cupcakesbydel
Linkedin.com/in/delphinedauphin

Delphine Nephtalie Dauphin is an 8-year-old owner of a high-end pop-up bakery, inspirational speaker, beginner pianist, ballet dancer, philanthropist and published author. Delphine resides in Miramar, Florida. She launched her cupcake business, Joy's Yummy Cupcakes by Delphine, on July 23rd, 2016, and serves more than 50 customers every weekend. She is a former Kidz Count Ambassador, whose mission is to empower the lives of our youth by equipping them with the financial literacy and the ability to create and sustain financial independence. She also serves as a royal ambassador of Princess and Pearls, an organization that trains girls on proper etiquette.

Delphine has exhibited her cupcakes at several events, such as the Miami Gardens Wine and Food Experience, Tri-Rail Fun Day, Produced with Purpose Children's Fair, Miami Book Fair, Little Haiti Book Festival and attended the Delta Sigma Theta Broward Chapter Alumni as a speaker, exhibitor and author.

Delphine added author under her little belt when she self-published I Am a Kid-trepreneur, a business guideline for kids by a kid.

Last summer, she conducted a three-part series of business workshops for FANM, the Haitian Women of Miami summer camp program.

Delphine has been featured in the Miami Herald Newspaper. Chokarella radio show, 1320 AM Radio, Rich Single Momma, Kids of the Cosmos, Creative Magazine and Miami New Times, to name a few.

Delphine is a Women's Empowerment nominee, and a Miami Book Fair presenting author. She has volunteered her time and talent to several nonprofit organizations. She has participated as a keynote speaker at kids' events, baked free cupcakes, fed the homeless, collected funds and supplies for underprivileged kids and donated to the Haiti and Puerto Rico relief. With all these accomplishments, Delphine has a well-balanced lifestyle and has educationally performed above 95% of her peers through national testing.

Delphine's mission in life is to inspire other kids to achieve greatness in whatever shape or form. Delphine lives by the belief that kids are not just the future, they are the present in motion.

What is your favorite quote that can be printed on a T-shirt, written on a mirror or wall?

- Okay. I have so many. Number one is, "If I can do it you can do it too" because I started my business and I'm still going. So, if I could do all this with my business at such a young age then you can surely do it.
- Number two is, "Anything is possible" because I tried it. I succeeded. It will never become possible if you don't try.
- Number three is, "Never give up," because I didn't get it right on my first try. I had to keep going. Number four is, "Try your hardest," because if the pressure is getting harder on you, go harder.
- Number Four is by Kevin Hart "My drive is other people's success."
- Number Five is by Will Smith "Greatness exists in all of us."
- My last one is "Now or never" Why wait on tomorrow when you can start now? What is stopping you from taking the step? What if today was a divine opportunity? Start now.

What are the 6 major ingredients or components that have contributed to the formulation of your success as a young change-maker thus far?

There are 6 major ingredients or components to the formulation of my success as a change-maker.

172

1. **Age,** because some people think that just because we're kids we can't really do anything. We are smart, we can create, we can own a business and we can change the world. A perfect example - I was a presenting author at a book fair. I was in the VIP/author's line and the attendants who were giving the entrance bracelets told me that the kids' line was on the other side. I replied, "Yes I know, but I'm supposed to be over here." Then they said, "No, because you're a kid You have to go over there." Finally, I said, "I am the author," and I pulled out my book. They still didn't get it. I pointed at their papers and said, "Look at the list, it's in there. My name is Delphine Dauphin." They looked at my book then the list and they found my name. It was there the whole time. They were a little bit embarrassed because they started to apologize "Oh I'm so sorry, Ms. Dauphin, please come right in." They wanted to know my story, how and why I started a business. They were calling other people to see this young author. "Do you know she has a business? Oh, do you know that she has a business? She has a big business and she's only just 8." no matter how old you are use your age as an advantage.

2. **Networking.** Everytime I meet someone and they hear about my business, they want to support and invest, therefore new doors of opportunities are opened. I am genuinely interested in other people's lives. I want to know how alike we are and how we differ. My number one goal in networking is to get to know the person. It's not about business, it's more of, "I am good at this and you are good at that. Our differences or our similarities can make the world a much better place." So, at the end of the day, they help me grow my business and I help them with whatever I can. If they want to start a business and they want some tips, I help them. Networking opens new doors for both parties.

3. **Mentors.** Everyone needs at least one mentor to help them. We are not perfect. Everyone needs help. I am blessed with some great mentors. Your mentors will help you with your business in the area that they are great in. The role of a mentor is to keep you accountable. A mentor serves like a coach or a counselor. Here are some of my mentors and their value to my success:
   - Public speaking / media training / finances / lots of love -- My mother is just great at giving me positive feedback and valuable tricks on how to develop my topic, and what not to do during interviews.

- Baking presentations -- I just call Ms. Elisha. She loves to help. She is a servant at heart. If I want to learn a new style of frosting or come up with a new design, she is there to teach me.
- Cheerleader -- My Grandma, Mrs. Prosper Hyacinthe is always so proud of my success. She is always cheering, "Go Delphine!" That makes me happy and makes me want to do better.
- Business goals – Ms. Ernisha is just awesome at getting me places. She doesn't care if people are saying that I am too young to be there. She believes that I have earned my place in the business world and that I am supposed to be part of business affairs.
- Etiquette -- Ms. Sonia Chess, OMG I just love her. She has been my mentor way before I had a business. She reminds me to sit up straight, and to wear my invisible crown every day. If I attend the Nickelodeon Choice Awards one day, I might need Ms. Sonia nearby.
- Spirituality / great life advice -- Pastor John Hyacinthe is my prayer buddy. Well, he is my uncle. He is a really cool pastor. He prays with me on the phone and he cheers me on all the time. That really builds my confidence and make me feel like I am here as a servant of the world.
- Empowerment -- Martha Benghie likes giving advice. She does not look at me as a little kid when it comes to business. I guess I take a little from her, because deep down, she loves business. I practice in front of her every day. Yes, I love to take her time. She enjoys it and gives me great advice on what to do when I am afraid. She challenges me all the time.
- Marketing/networking -- Ms. Suzan McDowell. Her reach is great. Like my auntie, she forgets my age, and I love it. She takes me places so I can network. She wants the best for me and my business. Did I mention that we were twins in a unicorn kind of way?
- Professionally -- Ms. Kenasha. She knows legal stuff. She gave me steps from the start of my business that I am still following. I will complete some of these steps this year.
Images – Mr. Attley Lawson. He is very nice at helping me with my pictures. He helps with concepts for great images. He has a business degree which is a great asset. He manages a great retail corporation, so I am learning a few things from him. My cover

page picture of this book is all him, I was just there to be photographed (smile emoji).

Do you see how great it is to have mentors? Start with one but as it goes along get some more. It speeds up the process. You don't really have to research some things if there is someone who can help you with it. Mentors don't do things for you. Mentors guide you to the door of success.

4. **Preparation** - I fix my bed before nighttime. In fact, I love to fix my bed in the morning and get it out of the way. If I come home tired, then I have nothing to worry about. It is the same in my business. I don't do things last-minute. I prepare, because if I don't, I'll be struggling. What if I have an "oops" moment? If I got something wrong or my cupcakes didn't bake right? I would have to restart again at the last minute. I don't like doing that, because then I will be in such a rush. But when I do things ahead of time and I have that "oops" moment, it's OK because I have plenty of time. I always have a plan for when one of my assistants calls out. What will my plan B or C be? You can never be too prepared.

5. **Education** - Business would not make sense to me if I were not doing well in school. I mean its sort of like the same thing, business and school, because you learn stuff and you do it. So, if I get an F in school, I'll get an F in business (my mom does not even believe in Bs). Trust me it's the same math, the same English or Creole or French or Spanish. You just have to apply it. Education comes first for me. I love to learn, and that reality helps me in business. I don't think my teachers would have approved of me doing business if I were not getting the grades. Every time I get my report card, it's just an assurance to keep doing what I am doing. The business is not affecting my schooling at all; in fact, it's making it better.

6. **God** - I love God. I feel like God makes things possible for me. Like when I go to an event, I always pray the Lord before I go on. It helps me succeed, and I know that God is looking over me and helping me. I'm just a regular kid who is doing something good - - great things if I admit. I fed the homeless and I was moved by the little kids I was helping. It brought tears to my eyes, but I was blessed to be put in the position were I can actually help. I was their inspiration and they were an inspiration to me. God is my guide.

What does your typical business or work day look like? When do you fit in fun, school, friends and family?

Well, my business operates from Thursday to Saturday. I have a system that I use in my business. On Wednesdays, I prepare my agenda for what my assistants are going to do. It works whether I am physically there or not. Sometimes I have play dates with my other friends, or I have an event to attend. I don't have to be there for them to do it. They know where the agenda is on the desk, they just follow through. My agenda lays out the whole weekend for my employees. Here's the brief version of my layout system: Thursdays, I have a brief meeting for about 5 minutes to go over the agenda and our goals. My assistant and I will go over the e-mails and look at our social media. I will supervise and work on the baking. I will frost the cupcakes once they're done, of course when they cooled down. I sign books that were ordered and get them prepared to be mailed out. Friday is usually more calls and deliveries. Saturdays are usually events and pop-up shops, and we close the day back at my office. Fun is a priority because my mother wants to make sure that I have a balanced life. God first, family, education, then fun. I hired three assistants because I didn't want to feel guilty during my play dates. Sometimes my assistants work on everything. Once, I went on a manicure play date with my friend, Laila. It was a little treat from her dad. I had lots of fun because business was being handled. It was done as if I was there because I have a system. My business does not get in the way of my relaxation or enjoyment. The hardest part is when one of my friends mentions to another my business background. It becomes a little hard to escape that conversation.

What would you say success means to you? Why is it so important?

Success is doing what I love and getting rewarded for it. I bake because it is what I want to do. Baking is something that I know how to do. When I bake, it's just like fun and I get to do what I love to do. Success is helping others achieve their dreams while you are on the ladder of success. Success is saving money for the future while you are still a child. Success is working smart and not hard. Success is when others think that you are successful, and you are just half way there. Success is giving with humility. Success is achieving your dreams with dignity. Success is using my platform to impact the world. Most of all success is self-love.

How important would you say it is to be connected to other young people doing amazing things? How did you make these connections?

I jumped on the idea when Zandra sent out this invitation actually. I think it's very important. Usually, young people admire other young people doing great things. So, if I have a business and say Zoey has a business, we can help each other because we are going through the similar challenges in our businesses. We can cheer each other on and help each other get better. At times, the parents could be a problem because they want their kid to be in the position that I am in, doing the things that I do. I have been a victim of that, and I ended up losing a friend because of the parents. I admired this group of people who I am collaborating with, because they are amazing to work with. They help build my confidence. They have my back like we're in a sorority.

How important would you say reading and research is to the success of your business? What 3 business books would you recommend?

Reading is very important. I am an early reader. I can read a book in just a few hours and then summarize it for someone. I love to read. It helps my writing. I learned big words that way. It expands my vocabulary. I even read the newspaper sometimes. The three business books that I recommend are:

I got bank! What my Granddad Taught Me About Money by Teri Williams. This book is written by the president of One United Bank, and it's about financial awareness for kids. I actually know Ms. Teri Williams, and that's how I got her book. Ms. Teri will be the right person to teach about money considering that she owns a bank. Valuable information in the book.

Jump by Steve Harvey. It helps me to take risks. It helps me to work on being OK in a room full of grown-ups. In *Jump*, it explains how you have to take a chance. If you want to create something, stop questioning yourself. If you want to play soccer, who cares if you are not good at it yet? Just jump. If you want to start a cupcake business, who cares if your frosting is not perfect? Just jump. You will master it eventually. The book is also an easy read.

Oprah: A Biography. She went through so much as a little girl and look at her now. She's helping other people with their problems even though she went through so much. She is such a success story. A story for the world to learn from. It would be selfish not to thank God, because I'm ahead of the game. I humble myself whenever I think of Ms. O.

I am a Kidtrepreneur is a must read, written by me, Delphine Nephtalie Dauphin. It's a business guideline for kids. It will help you set your business and be able to find success.

If you could advise a future young mogul to do 3 things before starting their business what would they be?

If I could advise a future young mogul to do 3 things, they would be research, system creation, and passion. You must have a little more than passion. You have to research the industry that you will be in. I have a specific television baking show that I love, and they were part of my research. I also had a movie that talks about the dynamic of friendships in business. You can never fail with research. Research everything, from the making of the product to the day-to-day aspect of the industry. If you research it then you'll actually know: It's like trial-and-error in science.

Then, create a system because I have my system for what I'm going to do as a kidtrepreneur. You must know what you want to do. How will you operate your business? You must know how often you will attend workshops in your industry. Your vision has to stay intact and must evolve as time passes. You will want to know what kind of employees to hire. You will want to know what collaborations you will embrace or reject. It's actually very important, because if you don't have a system other people will come up with unsolicited opinions about the administration of your business.

Lastly, passion is about 75 percent of this whole thing. At the end of the day, it has to be worth it. The only way for it to be worth the headache, the sleepless nights and the tears is for you to enjoy every aspect of your business. You have to be able to dance your way to it on most days. Your passion will not allow you to quit. Passion is contagious. If you are excited and joyful, others have no choice but to join in. Listen to me: Please do not look at what brings money, do not look at what your friends or enemies have, do something you love! My mother wished that I did something other than baking, but nope, that's what I love. I love to read, I love to bake and I love to write. Especially baking cupcakes because they're so delicious.

What are 3 lessons you have learned so far as a CEO, founder or public figure?

1. I have learned so many lessons in this entrepreneurial journey. Number one, I have learned that "no" is not a negative word. No just means "not this time," or that there is something better for me. It just makes me go to the next person and not waste time on them. I prefer a "no" over a "maybe."
2. Number two, it's harder than I thought that it would be. The success is moving faster than anticipated. The more opportunities that come my way, the more things not really related to cupcakes that I am doing. I knew that I wanted to change the world, but now it's like wow, I am really taking some great steps. Business gets tougher with legality. You have to make sure things are perfect legally.
3. Number three, it's OK to make mistakes. You just need to learn from them. Don't stress if you say the wrong word. Correct it if you can, or just learn from it. We are human, and we are not as perfect as we want to be, and that is OK.

Where do you pull inspiration from?

I pull my inspiration from DC Cupcakes. I love their bakery because I actually love how they do it. I love how they handle business. Do you realize how many times I use the word love? They show the struggles in business, what could happen and what does happen. They're so honest, and they love to do what they do. I get great tips from them.

My other inspiration is my mother. She builds my confidence and she tells me to try my best and never give up. She tells me never to put my head down. She wants me to always go after what I want after I strategize. I watch her work very, very hard. I watch her do excellent things. She puts my needs first every time. She is allowing me to live my dream. I see her by my side supporting my dreams. She helps me with my business. She takes me to my ballet and piano lessons and waits for me with a smile. She takes me out to nice restaurants. She makes sure I have full control over my business money. She teaches me how to balance it all. There are other people who do great things for me, but no one can be compared to my Mommy. No one.

What are 3 specific challenges you have had as a young mogul? How have you been able to overcome them?

Number one is proving that I am more than my age. I know my business in and out. You don't have to talk to an adult to get the answer that you need. Whenever someone asks my mother a question about my business, her answer is, "Well, I will ask Delphine." She does that because it's my business and I have the final say. The weirdest thing is that some people automatically think that the business belongs to an adult. They don't think that kids can actually start a business or do anything important. I am constantly having to prove myself. If kids can't attend the function then my business can't because I am the business.

Number two is the law. The law is not giving kids enough power and I get it. Why can't my name be on a bank account if I am the owner of the business? I think this should change where it requires both signatures (the parent and the child) because that's just not right. We're the ones who are doing the business and everything for the business. Kids in business need some of these laws to be changed. We want more rights.

Number Three. People comparing my prices with store-bought items. Huh, excuse me? I baked this from scratch, handmade. They don't go to Macy's and ask why their prices are higher than some other shops, yet they want to do this to me. No, I work hard in my business and that is my price.

What are your goals for the future? What's next?

I have so many, I can't even count. Well, I'll just start from the beginning. One, my non-profit organization, because I want to help young kids start their own businesses. I want to help the poor, and I want to help the homeless. I am already doing these things with the little that I have, but I want to take it up a notch.

Number two, my cupcake experience boutique. I want to have my own experience boutique because I want to have my little bakery, birthday party rooms and workshop areas. I want to start virtual classes to help other kids learn how to bake and start a business.

Number three, visiting Haiti. I want to visit Haiti and I want to actually help the kids in Haiti. I have been interested in helping my parents' land since the hurricane happened. I feel like kids there need to have an early business start like I did. I am not going there for a pity party. I am going there to collaborate with other kids at every economic level. These kids are so smart. I have two close cousins around my age who live there, and they speak three languages. That's just awesome to

180

me. Imagine if they have an early start in business, they will turn the world upside down then back up. Number four, I want to write another book, ***On the Paths to Success: After You Start a Business.***

Remember, it's never too early to start, because kids are not just the future, we are the present in motion.

My name is Delphine Nephtalie Dauphin. I am a CEO, business owner, Kid-Trepreneur and published author. I started my business at 7 years old. My mission is to inspire my peers and others to turn their passion into wealth. In my business I help people find joy in every bite of their customized yummy cupcake. In my book, I help people distinguish their passion, turn their hobby into a business, create a marketing plan that works and solve business challenges. I also am an inspirational speaker, a kid- business workshop instructor, a pastry chef, a ballet dancer, a pianist and a philanthropist. I hope to be able to work with you and help you achieve your success goals.

ACKNOWLEDGEMENTS

A very special thank you to those who have supported my journey and helped me turn my dreams into a reality...

Attley Lawson; Martha Benghie Hyacinthe; Reverend John Wesley & Doctor Genita Hyacinthe; April Jones & Autumn Gibbs; Emmanuela, Widopson & Wyatt Lormeus; Taina Caine; Marguerite Herzulia Hyacinthe; Suzan McDowell; Harold J. Dauphin; Myrline Oscar; Nowrin Alam; Eileen D'Ambrosio; Tamara Fleurimont; Wenda Oscar; Miguel Romain; Sthefie-Ted; Honore & Rodeleine Charlot; Adline Samuel; Bensy Dieujuste; Pooja Joshi; Nephtalie; Hyacinthe; Rosemary Tetteh

The Conclusion

This book has been about the magic of formulating your own success - the science behind it. The key to success is to take what you have learned or relearned in this book and put it into action. I know you got a lot of information from a lot of amazing young moguls. Think of this book as a road map, as a guide, an inspiration journal. Keep it next to your bed, in your bookbag or on your desk. Whenever you feel like it's too hard for you, or you feel like you're not being understood, you feel like you're alone in the world or you feel like giving up, remember that there is a science behind it.

Let me close with a few final thoughts. I want to remind you that these are things that can take you really far and very high along your journey, whether you're building an empire or a business. You're going to be the next king or queen in the pageant. You're launching a book. You're getting ready to write your first song, make your first piece of jewelry or hit the stage as an amazing speaker. Don't forget to ask for what you want. Always stay true to your craft. You have to learn to develop a habit of challenging yourself daily to always persevere. Remember to forever connect your work to your passion. Remember to always connect your work to a purpose and love beyond yourself. Be respectful and obey your elders and parents, but don't ever be afraid to ask questions. Now, I encourage you to go get started. Go do something amazing. Remember that you could very well be somebody's answered prayer. If you don't start today, there's somebody in the world who will won't be blessed by your product or service. Don't let anybody ever tell you that you don't have value and that you're not an amazing contributor to society. My co-authors and I have done the best we could to give you our secrets to success, the formula, if you will. We shared a few tools that you will need to go and make all of your dreams come true. These formulae, these ingredients, these components to success have made me what I am today. They have gotten me into doors that I've never imagined, sitting on couches that I never thought I'd sit on, as well as on many TV shows, radio interviews and podcasts. All over the world I have traveled and stood on stage speaking to hundreds of people.

Now you have it. The formula. The science behind it